ISBN 978-1-334-90208-6
PIBN 10779993

1 MONTH OF
FREE
READING

at

www.ForgottenBooks.com

By purchasing this book you are eligible for one month membership to ForgottenBooks.com, giving you unlimited access to our entire collection of over 1,000,000 titles via our web site and mobile apps.

To claim your free month visit: www.forgottenbooks.com/free779993

English
Français
Deutsche
Italiano
Español
Português

www.forgottenbooks.com

Mythology Photography **Fiction**
Fishing Christianity **Art** Cooking
Essays Buddhism Freemasonry
Medicine **Biology** Music **Ancient
Egypt** Evolution Carpentry Physics
Dance Geology **Mathematics** Fitness
Shakespeare **Folklore** Yoga Marketing
Confidence Immortality Biographies
Poetry **Psychology** Witchcraft
Electronics Chemistry History **Law**
Accounting **Philosophy** Anthropology
Alchemy Drama Quantum Mechanics
Atheism Sexual Health **Ancient History**
Entrepreneurship Languages Sport
Paleontology Needlework Islam
Metaphysics Investment Archaeology
Parenting Statistics Criminology
Motivational

Logic
Taught by
Love

Rhythm in
Nature and in
Education

By

MARY EVEREST BOOLE

Author of
"Symbolical Methods of Study,"
"Logic of Arithmetic," "Preparation of the Child for Science," etc.

1905
LONDON
C. W. DANIEL
3, AMEN CORNER, E.C.

ANY creature will follow a truth as long as he thinks that it will lead to something which he can approve. And what he will approve will depend on the accidents of his evolution.

He alone attains to the true dignity of man, who follows reverently in his thought whatever in practice he most disapproves, whenever it seems likely to lead towards Truth. Such an one has risen superior to accident ; and is, himself, an Evolver.

Dedication

To a Jewish Reformer

DEAR SIR,

WHEN Naaman the Syrian returned to his own people, after his memorable visit to the Land of your forefathers, he felt that Truth would seem to him, in later years, less like an impossible dream if he might make his offerings to the Eternal on an altar constructed of that sacred earth over which had trodden the feet of the Reformers of Israël. The Prophet, true to his function as a messenger from the All-Father, respected an instinct which of course he, personally, could not understand. May I ask you to tolerate a statement which certainly you will not understand? You have been to more than one writer on mathematical Logic the witness that fervent devotion needs no superstition about persons or observances, but may be kindled by reverence for the Creator Who works by laws of orderly causation. This faith of Science, we are often told, is necessarily loveless and cold ; there can be no fervour, it is said, without superstition or illusion. But where your influence reaches, all cherished illusions loosen their hold on the emotions ; for their beauty fades in the glow of your impassioned love of Truth.

Contents

Preface

THIS book will seem to some a mere medley. Is it a text-book of Logic, a pious exhortation, or a treatise on Mythology? Why cannot the author choose some plan and stick to it?

For this reason (among others): Part of the very object of the work is to call attention to the fact that our life is being disorganized by the monotony of our methods of teaching. To escape this monotony, we are driven to seek the needful variety in multiplicity of subjects of study and in conflict of opinion. Variety we must have; but we could get it more safely by alternation of attitude and variety of treatment.

The most important truths are those which no one disputes; but they are now too much forgotten, precisely because, not being disputed, and being monotonously taught, they are found uninteresting. In old days these truths were impressed on the mind by giving variety to the manner of their exhibition.

An eminent Logician says of his own work: "I am proud of having written a book on Logic, in which it is proved, among other things, that the Logic of the heart has its own validity." I should be proud if I could convince a single teacher that the isolation of any mode of thought is misleading; and that no system of Logic can be valid unless it is able to focus together various rays of Truth.

The substance of this Volume appeared in Articles in the *Inquirer*, *Journal of Education*, *Jewish Chronicle* and *Jewish World* of London, the *Occident* of Chicago, and the *American Israelite* of Cincinnati.

My best thanks are due to the owners of the long-lost Wedgwood MSS. (recovered in 1882), for confiding them for a time to me. These MSS. would not, it is thought, appeal to a sufficiently wide circle of readers to make the publication of them desirable; but they supply the missing link between the Pulsation-Logic of Gratry and Boole, and the most advanced medical psychology of our time.

Preface

Though I should be sorry to seem to commit any one to my views, I cannot refrain from also expressing my gratitude to those who have kindly helped me in tracing the effects of Jewish discipline in promoting personal and racial longevity ; amongst others, the Principals of Jews' College and the Jews' Free School ; the Editors of the *Jewish Chronicle* and the *Jewish World;* and, last but not least, my kind and valued friend, Mr. Lazarus, late Beadle of the Berkeley Street Synagogue.

The descriptions of lessons on elementary mathematics which occur on pp. 117, 118, 119 and 122 appear also in "The Preparation of the Child for Science."

M. E. B.

Logic Taught by Love

CHAPTER I

IN THE BEGINNING WAS THE LOGOS

WHAT creative Energy is, in Its own Nature, we do not know; It is The Ineffable I AM. What we do know about It is the fact that It pulsates. The very life of all that lives consists of some mode or other of Pulsation or alternate action. Without this Pulsating action, nothing grows. As the old writers said, It was in the world, and the world obeyed It by compulsion but knew it not. Then It made man, free to know It. Man, being free, sought out many inventions, all intended to substitute some fixed condition for incessant pulsation in human affairs; and to substitute the worship of some fixed entity for that of the Eternal Pulsator. But to some few the secret Wisdom revealed Itself; and to them IT gave power to become Sons of God. And all the History of religion, of morals, and of Philosophy, is a history of conflict between the Seers who would teach the Law of Pulsation and the multitude who would pervert their teaching.

All Life is pulsation; and health is always rhythmic pulsation timed in accordance with the proper rhythm of the particular organ. Every baby's lungs learn this at their first contact with the air; the baby-heart has caught the secret long ago by sympathetic contagion from its mother's heart. Nature teaches her mighty secret to the baby heart and lungs; and leaves the "voluntary muscles" and the brain to learn it voluntarily. We have gone but a little way yet towards finding out how to do this; still the gymnast knows that much may be done towards hardening limbs against fatigue and disease, by a regular rhythmic alternation of extension and contraction; and logicians such as Gratry (and much greater men before him) knew that, to a large extent, the same can be done with the mental faculties. The future possibilities that open out before us as we study the great Logicians of the Pulsation doctrine, are overwhelming; one hardly dares realize all that they imply; but the fact is, that the heart and lungs do actually sing in their own language, the Eternal Hymn —Holy, Holy, Holy is the Logos, the Hidden Wisdom, the Principle of Rhythmic Pulsation, which was in the beginning, is now and ever shall be, Creator of all that is, Preserver of what has proved itself worthy, Purifier by the destruction of all that is sluggish or disorderly. The goal to which we are tending seems to be to train all our faculties, one after another, to take their parts in the same Chorus. The very antagonism of the masses to the teachers of Pulsation is a suspension which enriches the Harmony, the means by which is created the possibility of the Highest Rhythm. Humanity toys and coquets with its own bliss; it dares not let itself know what the Logos has prepared for those who love Him.

For no one really doubts the doctrine of Pulsation. Every new birth is a witness to the truth that *conception* (whether physical or mental) is the result of re-uniting at a suitable moment elements that have been suitably differentiated. We all know it; but we fear to let ourselves believe.   History, as the Apocalyptic Seers knew, is the story of the alternate withdrawal of man's mind from the Logos-doctrine and re-union with it.

That perennial Love-Story has been intertwined with another, not less solemn and vital.   Far back in the ages a Tribe was differentiated, to be to the other races of the earth what the Unseen Logos is to Humanity as a whole; the subject of incessant misunderstanding; and the object of alternate fear, dislike, contempt, and superstitious reverence.   We never understand the People of Israël (nor can it be said that they ever rightly understand us); but every now and then we are made to feel that some magnetism is coming forth from the incomprehensible Race, which acts as a solvent to our metaphysical perplexities; which is the witness to and preparation for a Life higher than anything we can conceive.

The complex and variable relation between Jews and Gentiles, so unutterably sweet in some aspects, so bitter often, so unsettled and incomprehensible always, seems to be one chief means by which Humanity is being made fit for the rapture of intelligent comprehension, and able to look into the Face of Love.

The Race of Israël is the hereditary priesthood of that Unity whose action is Pulsation.   There is another such priesthood: occasional, unrecognized, consecrated by no hand but that of suffering, marked out by no special observance except that of being always peculiar everywhere; High Priests for ever after that order to which all official priesthoods are forced, sooner or later, to do homage.   Out of the deeps they have called; and Truth has heard.   Where steady health sees solid things and enduring systems, the *sick* often perceive, instead, a shimmering palpitation.

The man of whom it is said that he made the greatest advance in Logic since Aristotle, said of himself, that no one could do certain kinds of work unless he would *consent to be ill.* The majority decide, of course, that the perceptions of illness are "abnormal"; in old days these abnormal perceptions were called "miraculous." The name matters little; the important thing for us is to see that we do not waste the gifts that God sends through suffering.

Jesus, the High Priest of Pulsation, offered himself to death rather than support any one-sided rights or any fixed doctrine. And having been slain by one set of idolaters, He was made into the object of sensational worship by another set. And now, as ever, the teachers of the Eternal Logos are alone on the earth; and yet we are not alone, because the Father is with us, and all the Seers who went before us.

If we sorrow overmuch about the idolatry of our brethren, do not we thus prove ourselves to be also idolaters who would arrest the natural Pulsations? For the conflict between Seers of New Truth and the lovers of fixed ideas is the very palpitation of human life, the great witness to the doctrine that progress takes place by pulsation.

In some of the following Chapters an attempt is made to picture past episodes in the conflict between the Logos-Seers and their antagonists; in others, suggestions are offered of means whereby that very conflict might be converted into an orderly and peaceable mental gymnastic.

CHAPTER II

THE NATURAL SYMBOLS OF PULSATION

Heaven and Earth declare the wonder of His Work.

THE History of early religions is very much a history of the successive introductions into public worship of various symbols, by means of which the Seers hoped to make the masses realize the perpetual Flux or Pulsation which underlies the phenomena of Nature. The Seer perceives the Law of Pulsation by observing a certain phenomenon; that phenomenon becomes for him interesting; he tries to make the masses share his interest in it, as a revelation of Nature's fundamental Law; the masses lose sight of the idea of pulsation, and get up an idolatrous (*i.e.* fixed) tension on the symbol itself. To the pure in heart who see the Logos, all things are pure, because all things suggest the ineffable " process of becoming"; and those things are naturally sacred to any man, and an object of religious reverence, which most vividly suggest it to him. But to the masses things are not thus pure; because they see, in each thing, not the Creative Logos, but some special quality which is, or which they suppose to ·be, the especial characteristic of that object. Each Seer tries to break up the association of special Sanctity which clings round the symbol employed by his predecessor; in all good faith and innocence he tries to teach Flux-doctrine by some new symbol; and so the process begins again. It has in various forms gone on throughout the History not only of religion, but of all the intellectual and moral life of the world; it is made intelligible by studying those natural objects which at various times have been associated with religious ceremonies.

The movements of the Heavenly Bodies revealed to the Seers some mighty Principle of rhythmic motion; those whom they tried to indoctrinate with this idea worshipped Sun and Moon and Stars. The Seers erected stones to facilitate consecutive observation of the heavenly motions; the people supposed those stones to be possessed of magic virtues. It would seem that at some time in the world's history the process of becoming was taught chiefly by reference to vegetable growth. The people attached fantastic ideas to the grotesque forms of certain vegetable objects. Then the Seers selected for use in teaching certain trees distinguished by the absence of tendency to grow into suggestive shapes, and which exhibit in a severely simple form the main laws of growth.[1] The idolaters constituted these particular trees or plants sacred. Then the Seers ordered the sacred plants to be burned in homage to the Unseen Cause of growth; the masses made an idolatrous ceremonial out of the very act of destroying a sacred Symbol. The Seers would seem then to have turned from the vegetable, which only grows, and whose growth can only be inferred, not seen, to the animal, in which the life-process reveals itself by visible motion. To the medical priest, who, by dissecting a ram's heart, has caught the secret of the throbbing of his own heart, the ram is henceforward a sacred object. The mass of mankind are, however, not easily interested

[1] Such is the characteristic of all the sacred Trees which I have been able to examine.

in abstruse and as yet imperfectly developed physiological theories; to them, a ram is—a beast of certain shape. They see his form, but not the pulsating force which constitutes his life; and, of all that the enthusiast has told them, they remember nothing, except that when they say their prayers they are to look at a ram. From that to the worship of a ram-god is an easy step for the unthinking multitude.

When the sacred beast dies, Superstition makes of him a mummy, so as to preserve as much of him as can be preserved. The Seer orders him to be burned in honour of The Unseen Giver of Life. The masses attach superstitious ideas to the very fire that consumes the offering. The Seer orders that part of the flesh shall be consumed, not by the fire, but by the very worshippers; the masses make the meal a superstitious observance. Some Seer tries to show that the important thing in the beast is not his death, but the lessons drawn from the palpitating entrails which reveal the secret of life; the next generation declares that the Prophet drew auguries from the entrails.

Another Seer tells how mere tension on the lessons of the past is idolatrous and barren, and mere following of one's personal inspirations is dangerous and misleading; that he alone is a true Prophet by whose head converge the two streams of instruction, inspiration and tradition, as two birds may fly from distant points of the horizon.[1]   Posterity says that the great man of old taught how to gather knowledge from the flight of birds.

And so on, ever round and round the same weary circle, the Seers rolling up the Sisyphus-stone towards

---

[1] Odin's birds were "Thought" and "Tradition."

true enlightenment; the masses ever plunging back into idolatry and carnalism.

There was in old times one practical difficulty connected with the conflict, which may well account for the eagerness of ancient Prophets to put an end to idolatrous conceptions. To every genuine philosopher the symbols of certain physical functions are among the most sacred of all objects, as being the perennial witness that the Logos is with man; and not with man only, but with all Creation. But the masses can see nothing in these objects except the symbols of certain pleasurable sensations; and if they are taught to think intently of them, they make their religion consist in the stimulation of mere sensation. This has been the cause of numberless disorders, and excuses much Prophetic injustice and bigotry on the subject of Idolatry.

The Founders of Judaism desired that the People should be taught, as far as possible, by symbols possessing in a very marked manner the property of *evanescence*. The Sun and Moon, the symbols of pure Light, had been degraded to idolatrous purposes; Moses seems to have tried to make his people feel that some phosphorescent material, which shone only rarely, was more truly sacred than the Sun and moon. In fact, the Mosaic religion may be described as one which abjures, as far as possible, the consecration of colour-and-form manifestations which are either *partial* or *permanent;* it takes, for its principal symbols, manifestations which are essentially evanescent; and it keeps permanently enshrined nothing but revealed Laws. The writer of Genesis asserts that the true symbol of God's covenant with Man is the Rainbow; which no man can capture or embalm or enshrine; which is made by the occasional breaking-up of the One Light into many colours, to fade before long into the Unity of White Light again; and which, when it departs, leaves nowhere in the world a trace of its having existed, except on man's heart an impression of spiritual beauty, and in his mind the power of attaining a knowledge of the Laws of Light.

We gain a curious side-light on the early history of religions by the study of Cornish legends. When, in the early ages, savage tribes were converted by strangers of a different religion, the priests who converted them taught them to connect the memorials of their old faith with the idea of *evil magic*. Where, therefore, we find Druidic stones, believed by peasants to be relics of evil magicians, we may guess that some conversionist has been trying to indoctrinate people with his views. In Cornwall there are distinct traces of a stratum of some religion intervening between the old idolatry of fixed stones and the Christian ideas imported from Rome through England. The characteristic of Cornish legends is that monoliths are people who would not pay proper respect to the Sabbath; and who, as punishment for that crime, were arrested on their way to somewhere where they wanted to go, and were struck into stone to stand on the moor for ever, to show what comes of not keeping Sabbath. Now when we know about any preacher, that he instructs his flock to expect, as the penalty for neglect of religious observances, *arrestation of progress*, and *the falling into a permanently fixed position*, we can form a tolerably clear idea what was the main character of the religion taught by him. we are not here, however, left dependent on mere inference, for the religious teachers who converted the Cornish from their early idolatry left behind them another trace besides the legend of the people who would not keep Sabbath.   In contrast with these evil stones, there are others held sacred by the peasants almost to our own day ; the so-called " logan-stones." A logan-stone is one so delicately poised, that a child's touch can make it sway to and fro ; yet it presently returns to a position of equilibrium by virtue of its natural equipoise.   The name "Logan" is derived from a word in use in Cornwall, to "log" *i.e.* to *sway, rock, vibrate.*   We need not ask what was the philosophy of teachers who held sacred the logan-stone.

Perhaps the most impressive of all Natural Symbols of progress by Pulsation is the one referred to by Jesus —the Law of the circular Storm, which might be suggested to any true lover of Nature by observing the wheeling dust.   The Spirit which guides man is like the whirling wind; it blows backward in one place while it is blowing forward in another ; so that you cannot tell in what direction it is going as a whole, merely from feeling how it blows on you.

In connection with this subject I may mention a remark that has occurred to me in reading works of piety.   All sorts of religious writers agree in describing the troubles of life as " stormy seas."   The instinct of some leads them to speak of taking refuge from the storm in an *Ark* (which sways with the heaving sea, and yields to its every motion); while others, on the contrary, prefer to think of clinging for safety to a fixed stone or cross, or other immovable object.   The writers of "clinging" symbolism are of the properly orthodox type; if such a man should happen to disagree with the ecclesiastical superior who is in authority over him, it will be owing to the disturbing accident of some other having gained a stronger hold on his mind. But the man who, like Baxter, writes hymns about taking refuge in an Ark, is normally a heretic by the very nature of his mind; a natural Free-thinker, born to be a reformer and an Apostle of the Hidden Logos. There are, indeed, some who express the sense of trust in God without reference even to an intervening Ark; they find sufficient security in the very Law of the Storm itself. He who is scientific enough to know the rhythmic pulsation which is revealed in the Law of the Storm, feels sure that it will cease when the appointed time has come. Suggestions of this feeling are common in the Hebrew Scriptures; the following is a modern English instance :—

> " O'er this fair and blooming earth,
>   When the rushing storm has birth,
>   And the wingèd lightning flies,
>   And the tempest rends the skies,
>   And the sea with deafening roar
>   Rolls its strength along the shore ;
>   Yet within its limits' bound
>   Raves that storm its little round.
>   O'er the flood Jehovah reigns,
>   Ever He a King remains.

> " From the sphere of human things,
>   When Peace waves her parting wings,
>   Bidding mighty Nations quail
>   At the Future's opening veil ;
>   Famine lift her withered hand,
>   Battle waste a sinking land,

Social warfare, civil strife,
Wither all the flowers of life ;
Yet within its bounds assigned
Is that tempest's wrath confined ;
And in limits sealed and set
Human passions roll and fret ;
O'er the Water-flood Who reigns
Evermore a King remains.

" When above my fainting head
Gathering clouds of ill are spread,
Wild and dark the Heavens around,
Rough my path on alien ground ;
Still, O Lord of Hosts, in Thee
Shall my trust unwavering be ;
For the dwelling of Thy Throne
Is where tempests are unknown ;
And Thy sceptre and Thy sway
All life's waves and storms obey ;
O'er the Water-flood Who reigns
Evermore a King remains."

GEORGE BOOLE.

CHAPTER III

GEOMETRIC SYMBOLS OF PROGRESS BY PULSATION

" When He made a decree for the rain, and a way for the lightning, He saw Wisdom ; and to man He said, The fear of the Lord is Wisdom."
—JOB xxviii. 26—28.

WHILE such Seers as Moses, Isaiah, and Odin were struggling to make the masses attend to the Genesis of things, or process of becoming, to give them some sort of faith in the very existence of any Laws of moral development by reaction, certain thinkers of less actively social and philanthropic temperament retired into solitude to study those Laws in detail, and to impart their knowledge to a few chosen pupils. Many of them studied the Laws of mental development by the method of mathematical analysis. The vulgar called such students Wizards and other harsh names. The pursuit of mathematical Logic was often forbidden; the books of "Grammarye" were burned; and sometimes the writers and readers of them. At other times Wizards were held in high honour. Is it not possible that the famous breast-plate of Aaron, which was consulted in mental difficulties, may have had inscribed on it a selection of the Natural and Geometric Symbols of orderly mental sequence?

In modern times it has been assumed that the study of mathematical Logic must have been "mystical" or "fanciful." But in the middle of last century the Science was revived by a group of writers, among the foremost of whom may be mentioned Babbage, De Morgan, Gratry, and Boole. These philosophers have reclaimed us from bondage to the ignorant dictatorship of the opponents of "Grammarye," by proving that all the more important thought-processes can be illustrated Algebraically. Whatever can be stated in Algebraic symbols may legitimately be expressed, so far as possible, by mechanical action, or in diagrams. The practical possibilities of Algebraic notation are, it is true, far wider than those of mechanical or pictorial representation; but, when a truth has once been expressed Algebraically, it can no longer be considered fanciful to illustrate, by motion or by diagram, as much of it as is capable of such illustration. We are therefore free to teach the elements of the Higher Logic, to those unacquainted with the notation of Algebra, by the same methods as were used of old in schools of Free-Masonry and of Prophecy.   Messrs. Benjamin Betts and Howard Hinton are creating a simple system of representation, by the use of which the study of Logic by diagrams will some day be carried much further than has ever yet been possible.   In this Chapter I propose to give some idea of the elements of the Science which teaches geometrically the laws of mental Pulsation.

A stone, escaping from a sling, exhibits tangential motion, overcoming the counteracting force of the string. According to modern definition, tangential momentum is not, properly speaking, a Force.

" Let knowledge grow from more to more, yet more of reverence in us dwell; " reverence for the Light vouchsafed to those who had not our advantages in the way of technical knowledge.   To the thinker of the far back ages, these were the facts presented as a basis for speculation :—

If he dropped a stone from his hand, *something* made it fall at once, straight towards the earth.   If he put it in a string and whirled it, *something* prevented its either falling as far as the string would allow, or yielding quite freely to the pull of the string.   If it escaped from the string, *something* made it fly, not straight to the earth, but off towards the distant horizon.   What were these rival somethings ?   Were they warring dæmons ?   And was his string a magic implement which altered the balance of power between these unseen personalities ?

If the thinker was a Hebrew Prophet, his doctrine of Unity provided him with an answer.   The various phenomena were not the work of rival personalities, but various manifestations of the Dunamis or Power exerted by The Unity Who speaks through diversities. And when his confidence in that Unity had given him skill to conquer an opponent, both more richly endowed by Nature than himself and more amply provided with material and mechanical appliances (of learning?), he went back to his sheepfold and sang under the silent stars: "Oh! how love I Thy Law; all the day long is my study in it." The knowledge of Science possessed by the ancient Hebrew was no doubt very elementary; but perhaps it does his more fortunate European successor no harm to reflect that, so far as it went, it was sound. Nor is it bad for the over-cultured, over-specialized, over-examined little victims of advanced education to have their hearts brought into sympathy with the emotions of the Sacred Past, while their fingers are handling its implements, and their intelligence is brought into contact with its problems. The practice of playing with such toys as the sling and stone, the sucking-valve, the old-fashioned rope-maker's wheel, and the bandalore, may be made a means of accustoming children's nerves to the feeling of Nature's opposing tendencies, and may prepare the organization for receiving knowledge, later on, into the conscious mind. By training the hand to trace out Nature's action, we train the unconscious brain to act spontaneously in accordance with Natural Law; and the unconscious mind, so trained, is the best teacher of the conscious mind.

Another interesting exercise is that of tracing the Pentagram. Number the angles of a regular Pentagon in order; and draw straight lines from 1 to 3, from 3 to

5, from 5 to 2, from 2 to 4, from 4 to 1. Repeat several times in succession. Choose the size of the Pentagon to suit the size of the hand. After some practice, the Pentagram should be drawn by freehand. The exercise may be varied by tracing the Heptagram, *i.e.* passing from one point to another of a regular Heptagon in this order—1, 4, 7, 3, 6, 2, 5, 1. Childish as the foregoing description may seem, the tracing of these figures gives a curious *feeling* of arriving at completeness, by a series of tentative Pulsations backwards and forwards; and in old days the idea of magic attached itself to the exercise. At a time when the ability to investigate the angles of the Pentagram represented a high degree of mathematical skill, we may imagine that some enthusiast, in a fit of that tender fun which is characteristic of scientific genius, conceived the idea of tracing the figure on his threshold, saying to his pupils, " No lying spirit can enter, nor can science degenerate into sorcery, if study is put under the safe guardianship of accurate mathematics. Very slight inaccuracies," he would add, "leave room for the entrance of any kind of treachery and deception." Later on it came to be believed that drawing a Pentagram on the threshold of a study prevented Satan from entering, provided it were drawn with sufficient accuracy. If at any point the junction were imperfect, the devil entered through the gap! The process by which the Pentagram degenerated from being the symbol of a scientific accuracy which shields from temptation to duplicity, into being a magic weapon of defence against a personal devil, is typical of all such degradations.

We now pass from the Science which teaches Natural Law by training the muscles, to that which addresses itself more directly to the intellect, and through the intellect to the soul.

The reform in the teaching of mathematics, now in agitation, depends essentially on getting teachers to understand that the chalk in the lecturer's hand becomes, at a given moment in the lesson, a Revealer, independent of (and, for the moment, superior to) the man who holds it; a Teacher of Teachers, King of Kings, and Lord of Lords.   Yet how easily this essential doctrine of mathematics slips over into the slavish dogmas which ignorant people connect with the so-called doctrine of Transubstantiation!   And how wisely did the English Church decree that the "transubstantiated" bread shall be eaten at once, not preserved as sacred!   We do not wish the children to attach superstitious ideas to the chalk (or bread) when the demonstration is over; but if there is to be any vital reform in method we must make young teachers realize that, for a few moments in each lesson, he and the chalk *change* places; that for those moments the chalk, not he, is the true intermediary (or mediator) between the Unseen Revealer and the class.   We cannot continue to boycott in England all vital mathematical teaching, just because stupid people have talked grovelling nonsense about the doctrine which is its vital essence.

The manner in which a problem that baffles us when treated on its own level can often be solved by bringing to bear on the solution truths of a higher order than that contemplated when the question was first propounded, is well illustrated by the famous 47th Proposition of Euclid.   The question proposed for solution is this:—
Is there any constant relation between the length of

the hypothenuse of a right-angled triangle and the lengths of the sides? We are now so familiar with the solution, we have so mechanicalized the process by which the answer is arrived at, that the significance of both escapes us. But let us place ourselves, in imagination, back at the time when the question was as yet unsolved and was being eagerly investigated. In studying the earlier problems of Euclid, questions about lengths of lines are settled by striking circles with compasses (which is virtually a process of measuring); and questions of area, etc., by superposition. Everything is referred to certain axioms which act as a hurdle set up for the purpose of giving children the exercise of climbing over it. The formal Logic in the beginning of Euclid exercises a certain mental agility; but everything which is really found out, is found out by trusting to the evidence of our senses aided by some mechanical process.

But when we attempt to find a relation between the hypothenuse and sides of a right-angled triangle, all modes of measurement fail to show any fixed relation, *and appear even to show that none exists.* Those who were satisfied that nothing was valid except the evidence of the recognized instruments probably asserted that the existence of any fixed relation *was disproved.*

But there were true Free-Masons in those days, or rather there were Free Geometers, the founders of Free-Masonry; bold, untamable spirits, who dared invoke the All-Seeing Eye of the Great Unity to enlighten their blindness; and who well knew that rules limiting the play of the human intellect were made, chiefly, to be defied. They claimed the right to seek Truth outside the limits marked by orthodox compasses; they knew that, when we find our way stopped in the order of thought to which we have hitherto been confined, such experience is an indication that the time has come to investigate afresh the question of the relation between different orders of thought. By transferring the search for a relation between the hypothenuse and the sides to an order of dimensions *higher* than that involved in the original question, we find that there is a constant relation, one indeed of absolute equality, between the *square* on the hypothenuse and the squares on the sides.

Let us think with sympathy of the orthodox Geometricians. They thought, of course, that they had exhausted all the possibilities, and satisfactorily proved that the constant relation sought had no existence. And behold, here come dreamers, who claim the right to overthrow all established boundaries of knowledge; to evade difficulties by a mere trick; and to solve the question, declared unsolvable, by reference to some extra-linear order of ideas! We can well imagine their disgust. Alas for human short-sightedness! the defenders of orthodox methods are forgotten; and "the dreamers, the derided, the mad, blind men who saw" Truth, because they persisted in ignoring the cobweb barriers raised by intellectual timidity,—these heretics built the Temple dedicated by the Wise Man to The Great Unity; and they also founded the Geometry of the Future.

The moral of Euclid is this:—As long as we are investigating relations with no reference to any higher order of ideas than is obviously involved in those relations, we could make each discovery by some empirical method; a new order of thought begins at the point where we introduce into our reasoning considerations derived from an order of thought higher than that whose relations we are investigating.

Now the present condition of moral and religious reasoning is about on a level with that of mathematical reasoning at the time when a few bold spirits were proposing to look for an equation between lines in the region of non-linear surface; and the majority were expressing scepticism and indulging in sneers. The parallel is perhaps all the more accurate, because reasoning about lines as lines is in itself, and necessarily, in a sense illusory. There is no such thing in Nature as a line, except the edge of a surface (nor, indeed, can there be any surface except the boundary of a solid).

Thousands of years before any such definite conception dawned in mathematics as that to which the name "dimensions" attaches itself now, it must have occurred to thoughtful men to study the shadows cast by solid objects. The duration of the shadow, it would be observed, is not coeval with that of the substance from which it is projected; a passing cloud is sufficient to obliterate it. Nor is its form solely determined by that of the solid object, but partly by the position of the latter relatively to the Source of Light. Pondering on this would lead to experiments in shadow-producing. Of the exact course of the shadow-study carried on by wise men of old we have no accurate record; but whoever is engaged in prosecuting similar investigations now, is sometimes irresistibly made to feel that he is going over the same ground as has been trodden by some "inspired" writer of the olden time. To avoid controversy, I propose here only to indicate a simple method by which any person of average intellect can commence the shadow-study, and introduce children to it. The points of contact between us and the ancients, I shall (with one important exception) leave the reader to find out for himself. I will observe, however, that the shadow-study was a favourite amusement of George Boole; and it would appear from the Seventh Book of the Republic, that Socrates was familiar with it.*

Those who are only beginning the shadow-study can work most conveniently with a single light overhead. Later on, combined and crossed lights can be used, and in some cases it will be useful to have a movable light. Place on the table a sheet of white paper. Hold between the paper and the light a ring. Call attention to the fact that the same ring casts a *circular* or an *oval* shadow, or a straight line, according to the position in which it is held. Also that the same series of shadows is produced by an elliptical ring as by a circular one. Either can be made to cast a shadow resembling in shape the other. A straight line, however (a knitting-needle for instance), cannot be made to cast a curved shadow on a plane; its shadow is always a straight line, which becomes shorter as the needle is tilted up, till at last it resembles a mere dot.

If a circular disk of card-board be held horizontal under the light, it can be made to cast a series of shadows resembling in turn each of the conic sections (circle, ellipse, hyperbola, and parabola), by altering the position of the paper on which the shadow is cast. The same series of forms may be produced by placing a

---

*This detailed account of the use of these symbols for educational purposes will be found in " The Preparation of the Child for Science." (Oxford : Clarendon Press).

lighted night-light in the bottom of a tall jar, and throwing the shadow of the rim of the jar on surfaces held in different positions.

The best paper to use is that which is ruled in small squares (it can be procured at the shops which furnish educational apparatus). The paper may with advantage be laid on the table with its lines pointing to the cardinal points of the compass; so that a line of shadow can be described by stating, *e.g.*, that it crosses so many squares from north to south, and so many from east to west.

Take a corkscrew-wire, with rings sufficiently large to throw a distinct shadow. It is possible to hold it so that its shadow is a mere circle; in another position it makes a mere wavy line. An ordinary spiral wire is easily procured, and in practice is sufficient; but we shall gain more instruction about the play of Natural forces if we picture to ourselves what would be the effect of using a spiral whose rings are *elliptical*. I shall assume here that we are using an elliptical spiral. The wire itself will then represent the path of a planet in space; one of its shadows pictures the path of the planet round its sun or suns; another, the path of the whirling storm-wind, to which Jesus compared that of Inspiration.

Let us now place our (elliptical) spiral in such a position that it casts no shadow except an ellipse, and, for convenience of reference, let us agree that the longer axis points north and south. Let us picture to ourselves a tribe of microscopic creatures, whose true destiny should be to proceed upwards in the direction of the coil as a whole, and who have a blind but irresistible impulse to do so. They have no mode of ascending except along the wire; and no mode of expressing statements about distance, except on the paper. They have a vague, dawning consciousness of movement in the up and down direction, and of distance from the paper. In some, this consciousness of up and down is very much more developed than in others. In some it is so weak that they believe it to be mere illusion; in others so strong that they fancy all other modes of movement are illusion. But (we suppose) none can make definite *statements* about motion, except by reference to the lines on the paper. Progress upwards, therefore, is, for all of them, non-statable except in so far as it is connected with motion across the surface of the paper.

A group of them have climbed round a half-coil, beginning at the northern extremity of the longer axis; and have now arrived at its southern extremity. Their actual progress has been upwards, and amounts to half the distance between two coils; their expressed and apparent progress is the length of the longer axis of the shadow-ellipse on the paper. Whether any individual will be most conscious of his actual or of his recorded progress will depend on the condition of his individual consciousness. The condition common to them all is this:—Such progress as is actual is not recorded; and that which is recorded and registered is not actual nor permanent.

Every part of the progress which is registered will have to be unmade soon after it is made. Only that which is not registered is permanent. The particular group of creatures under our consideration first made some progress in a direction partly southward, but partly also eastward, away from the longer axis. Already they have had to unmake their eastward progress and come back to the longer axis.   They have still, however, been able to congratulate themselves on a considerable amount of progress southward; and the optimists among them no doubt set up a theory that, after all, true progress is southward, and the eastward motion was only an accidental concomitant of the southward.   But when the extremity of the long axis is reached, a terrible conflict sets in; the upward path is beginning to turn towards the *north*-west.   The southward progress, therefore, is being lost!   A most dramatic novel could be woven of the conflict of opinion and feeling that would arise, as soon as the nature of the situation came to be realized; for all the tragedy of History is summed up in the prosaic fact that " the actual progress is not statable; the recorded progress will all have to be unmade."

Whether the spiral wire was actually used in ancient times to teach the true principle of development, will perhaps never be known.   In this connection it may be well to notice that the Spiral of Ascent, the winding pathway, would naturally be represented to the early Geometrician (who lived where snakes were common and corkscrew wires not yet invented) by a snake coiled round a branch and hanging freely.   The Geometry of the snake-coil is a more advanced stage of the Logic of the Divining-rod.   In the fable of the rods that were shown to Pharaoh, the rods of both parties turned into snakes before that of the good prophet could swallow those of the bad magicians.

The Pentagram and the Magic Squares and other

puzzles used by ancient "Wizards" illustrate the same principle, though less clearly. The principle itself was well known to the writer of the narrative of Abraham's calling. Abraham lived at a time when children were recklessly sacrificed to the gods whenever the parent felt prompted to do so. First he saw there was something wrong about that; children were meant for something better than to be killed. Next, it occurred to him to think that he might be wrong after all; ought he not to hold himself ready to give his son to God if God willed? He prepared to obey—if God should will. Then he was led to see that God wills to accept the offering of our children in a different way; we are to offer them to The Unity; but so as to hold them in trust for the establishment of human society. Thus he was led gradually up the spiral of revelation; at each step giving up something which had seemed (though it had not really been) the essence of some previous revelation.

How Superstition has fastened on that standard narration of spiral progress, of which Abraham is the hero, it is hardly necessary to point out.

The whirling storm-wind forms an accurate diagram for illustrating the relation of the ex-centric to humanity. Having drawn the spiral, with tangents running in various directions, one tells the pupil that the spiral itself represents the methods of the orthodox Ecclesia, the constituted authorities, the recognized teachers. The tangents represent various paths taken by ex-centrics, non-conformists, men who have received the *first* personal inspiration, the first birth into a new world; who have cared, and dared, to go off on lines of their own, each investigating as he is impelled by his own genius.

That is very well for a time; the youth of genius should find out for himself what is the direction in which he is impelled to go. But before he offers his gift on the National Altar, before he can really contribute to the general store of Knowledge, he must pull himself into line with general progress. How shall he do this?

The advice usually given is, to conform to the general custom, submit to the orthodox authorities. But there is a better way. The normal to any tangent leads towards the centre of equipoise, of balance, of calm progress; the spot where is concentrated the maximum of force with the minimum expenditure of force in mere useless motion.

But how can any man find certainly the true normal to his own tangential direction, the path which will guide his own peculiar genius towards the centre of progress and of power?

The direction given by the diagram is emphatic and unmistakable. He should look out for the brother ex-centric who most especially "offends" him, who is going on what seems to him to be most obviously and certainly the wrong road, because it leads in the opposite direction to what he is sure is, for him, the path of inspiration. Let him unify with that brother, call out to that brother to meet him and join hands. When these two meet, they will be in the centre of calm force. This conversion into the normal is the second birth of genius, the Regeneration which converts mere inspiration into Revelation; for inspiration is at best partial;

Revelation comes at the moment of the combination of opposites.

As the spiral shows, all inspirations are inadequate; and nearly all are, in themselves, actually misleading.

A dim suggestion makes itself felt as we think of the spiral wire. The whole coil might, if long enough, be treated as if it were a wire, and wrapped in its turn round and round into a larger coil. We leave this consideration to the imagination of any reader who cares to pursue it. For none have more need of patience and reticence than those who are teaching the art of generalizing mathematical method, who are transferring to the analysis of ethics and history that knowledge of the human mind which is gained by mathematical investigation. All the various rays of light shed by our various studies came originally form One Source, and are meant to be re-united; but *not till the appointed time is come.* The danger of premature synthesis is that it leads to the vicious habit of what is called reasoning by analogy; jumping to conclusions about outer things and historical events. True analogy is of use as throwing light on *Laws of Thought;* it teaches, not Truth in itself, but *the nature of the relation of the human consciousness to Truth.* True Logic is not dogmatic about facts; it clears the ground of false conclusions, and leaves The Eternal Pulsation to speak in silence to the soul.

We now go back for a moment to the Tree-Symbolism. In the Hebrew Scriptures knowledge is spoken of as a Tree. In the Odin religion we are taught that: Its root is the knowledge of earth and its crown is the knowledge of Heaven.

CHAPTER IV

THE SABBATH OF RENEWAL.

" The Church bells were ringing,
  The Devil sat singing
On the stump of a rotting old tree:
  ' Oh ! faith it grows cold,
  And the creeds they are old,
And the world is nigh ready for me.'

"The bells went on ringing ;
  A spirit came singing,
And smiled as he crumbled the tree:
  'Yon wood does but perish,
  New seedlings to cherish;
And the world is too live yet for thee.'"

C. KINGSLEY.

EVERY now and then in History it has happened that
some isolated Seer has perceived afresh the vital connection between Mosaism (in the original intention of its
Founders) and the scientific doctrine of the renewal of
health by rhythmic pulsation. One of the most interesting instances of such perception is the Civil Engineer
Boulanger, who in the last century wrote a little volume
entitled, *L'Origine du Despotisme Oriental.*

The work is so advanced in tone that one can hardly
believe it is anything but a very clear summary of all
that has been discovered since the great French Revolution, about the respective effects of fixed mental
attitude in religion, and of free ventilation of religious
problems. It is not, however, an after-summary, but an
anticipation of modern investigations. The author
believed in a Creative Unity who is perpetually reveal-

ing himself to man. Every man who once places his feet firmly on that high vantage-ground, becomes (intellectually at least) a *Prophet;* that is to say, he is able to trace accurately the course of lights not yet arisen above the horizon of persons less fortunately placed. It seems to this writer natural and inevitable that whoever believes in the Divine Unity must be in advance of his age ; so much so, indeed, that he does not understand why the Jewish Prophets should be considered more inspired than other deep thinkers.

The true Revelation, he considers, was given before the invention of writing. The Bible is an attempt to perpetuate the memory of it by writing ; the rituals of savages aimed to do the same thing in a different way. Truth about religion and government will be brought to light whenever Judaism is frankly compared with the forest and cavern rituals. In fact, his mind seems to have been saturated with the idea that the germ of new Truth will always be found by following up two old strains of tradition to the point from which they originally diverged.

The second edition of the work is preceded by a letter of sympathy written by Boulanger to console a brother Philosopher who had been reviled and insulted by fanatics. He said that those who are too far ahead of their time to be understood should not puzzle contemporaries by the immediate publication of their ideas, but leave their work for posterity, who will be better able to appreciate it.

The key-note of the book is the intense conviction that despotism is only made possible by some form or other of idolatry, *i. e.* by the worship of some defined *part* of the great Unity. He has a horror of both tyranny and idolatry not unworthy of a Jewish Prophet. Yet he cultivates a genial sympathy with both tyrants and idolaters. No one, he believes, willingly invents an idolatry or imposes a tyranny. All such evils grow up by the degeneration of what was originally good. This degeneration, he thinks, might be prevented, if free access to all knowledge available at any epoch were given to all persons living at that epoch. The Prophets, he thinks, might have simply annihilated all false religions by explaining how they originated in natural and cosmical appearances. Why then give an apparent reality to the heathen gods by railing against them as if they were real? The true God would surely have found it as easy to convince idolaters as to punish them.

He who comments thus on the great men of the past, while professing to think that all accessible truth ought to be made available for all men, seems to have been keeping himself cool in his study, writing a treatise for the benefit of a possible posterity, who would need his instructions all the less for being already enlightened, while his contemporaries were, all around him, sunk in the most degrading slavery and superstition. He is criticizing men like Isaiah and Jeremiah, who had courage to enter into serious conflict with the vices of their own age, at all risk of disturbing the perfect balance of their own nervous systems. And here we find the answer to the question, why Isaiah was more truly a *Prophet* than Boulanger. A Prophet is a *plain utterer ;* *i.e.*, he not only sees truths ahead of his age, and thinks that the people ought to know them, but is so filled with the love of truth and right that he cannot lead a life of studious calm while self-interested charlatanism is misleading the masses; he feels that he must endeavour, at all cost to himself, to make what he knows accessible to whoever desires to learn it.   In other words a man is not, in the fullest sense, a Prophet, unless he is both an inspired Seer, and also an actual Re-former.   At all risk of over-balancing himself, such a man holds out a helping hand to whomsoever he sees falling into an abyss.   And perhaps few forms of human conceit are more cruel or more blind than the lack of sympathy shown by too many abstractly wise men towards mistakes into which practical reformers may temporarily fall.

Boulanger paid the natural penalty of his somewhat insincere optimism, and his lack of sympathy with the impassioned Prophets.   He committed himself to the prediction that tyranny and bigotry, and therefore the need for vehement resistance, were almost among the things of the past!   Thirty years after his death, the French Revolution exploded; proving that such Prophets as Jeremiah were not yet out of date.

To return to our author.   The Sabbath, he says, was originally a festival of renewal, the permanent memorial of a re-created world.   The Law of *Moses* means The Law adopted by a People saved from flood.   When a great misfortune has overtaken a country and des-troyed most of the population, the remnant who escape become, he says, for a time, serious and reverent; they try to express their gratitude for their preservation by re-organizing society in accordance with the will of the divine Law-giver as revealed in the laws of Nature.   But as the knowledge of Nature is, at any given epoch, incomplete, the compilers of human law supplement their lack of knowledge by framing provisional *working-*

hypotheses.   These hypothetical assumptions ought of course to be held lightly ; men ought to keep themselves always in readiness to substitute for any one of them any ascertained truth.   The tendency, however, of the untutored mind is always towards thinking fancy more sacred than fact, and doubtful episodes more divine than ascertained and eternal laws.   An instance of this perversion occurs in the history of the Sabbath.   Legislators who had discovered by experience the enormous importance to human welfare of a periodic rest from labour, wishing to enforce its observance, made a fanciful guess at the origin of the need which they perceived.   *Once upon a time, the Creator made visible objects on six of the days of the week, and abstained'from doing so on Saturday !*   Till somebody discovered a more intelligible explanation, it was hoped that this one would impress the Hebrew mind with the idea of keeping Sabbath. The average Hebrew mind fixed itself on the one fragment of fancy lying amid so much solid truth, with the tenacity of a barnacle clinging to a rock ; and alas ! with something of the short-sightedness of a barnacle, which supposes itself safe because it has got tight hold of a scrap of shell !   The Creator left off doing things on a certain Saturday long ago ; therefore it is very wicked to do *certain things on Saturday.*   (And indeed it is only too true that some Jews have so completely missed the essence of the Sabbath idea as to consider it wrong to carry an umbrella to Synagogue, but not wrong to sit at home thinking of accounts ; wrong to write a letter to an absent friend whom one has not time to correspond with in the week ; but quite permissible to " cram " for examinations at any subject which does not involve

holding a pen.) The true object of Sabbath, the pre-
vention of mental stiffening and moral hardening, the
re-creation of moral life by change of mental attitude, is
too often lost sight of; and many people know nothing,
and care to know nothing, of all the marvellous science
of periodicity by which the exceptional vitality of
Judaism has been created, except the one obscure and
doubtful statement, that, on one particular Saturday,
long ago, creative activity suspended its beneficent
operations!

And this is a fair sample of the manner in which what
once were religious truths degenerate into dogmas full
of superstition; the degeneration being in all cases due
to neglect of the study of antiquity. On this point our
author insists strongly. So far from the reverent study
of antiquity being a cause of superstition and a hindrance
to progress, it is the great preservative from the superstitions which grow up by the degeneration of useful
customs.

The refrain of the book is like the announcement of
a new day, a summons to awake to a richer and fuller
life. It is a mistake to suppose that *Sabbath* has any
necessary connection with inaction; the very words
Sabbath and *Jubilee* (the author insists) originally meant,
not *inaction*, but *renewal*. This message he leaves as a
legacy to posterity, who, he trusts, will be able to understand him. Cast thy seed upon the waters, and after
many days it shall be found!

Boulanger describes non-idolatrous religion by a series
of delicate negative touches, which, so to speak, chip
away, one by one, the elements of idolatry; leaving pure
religion to reveal itself.

"Idolatry does not consist, necessarily, in taking a statue, an animal, or a man, as the representative of God; to define it fully, we must say that every form of worship or code of law is idolatrous which takes as divine that which is not divine. It is not only idolatrous to treat a stone, or beast, or a mortal, as if it were God; we are also guilty of idolatry if we imagine that the words of that man, or the oracles pronounced through that statue are the very words and decrees of Deity. We are guilty of idolatry when we prefer speculations and mystical chimeras to reason and good sense; when we treat any legislative code as if it were dictated by the Almighty; when we endow with a divine character the servant of a theocracy; when we try to regulate the conduct of men here below by Laws suited only to Celestial beings; when we confuse heaven with earth; when we mistake our own position and pretend to be more than mortal; and when we forsake our own place as citizens of this world and subjects of the Civil Government, either to tyrannize over other men in the Name of God, or to live as recluses, despising or forgetting our fellow-men."

I have dwelt at length on Boulanger's charming little volume, because it affords a good example of the way in which rational views of the Scripture religion have occasionally been held throughout the ages, and have died out owing to the prevailing ignorance about the logical basis of the doctrine of progress by gradual Inspiration.

CHAPTER V

"Hilkiah said, I have found the Book of the Law in the House of the Lord."—2 KINGS xxii. 8.

TO form any adequate conception of the situation in which the founders of the modern pulsation-Logic found themselves, we must imagine a state of things somewhat of this kind.

Suppose that in some social convulsion, every ophthalmoscope were now to be destroyed, and all the men who use the instrument were to perish, leaving behind a few of those who had been accustomed to see it used, and to clean or otherwise handle it. We must suppose a great many ophthalmoscope-drawings preserved, with notes proving that these purported to be drawings of the retina.

After society had settled down again, the drawings might begin to attract attention. Thereupon would set in fierce discussion in the medical world. There would be a *tradition* that certain medical draughtsmen of the 19th century had a means of knowing what the living retina looks like; a means not accessible to ordinary men. Traditions would be handed down that the condition necessary for seeing how to do the drawings was *induced* by holding to one's eye a certain machine. These traditions would be different in form, according as the servant in whose recorded reminiscences it had originated had been accustomed to see his master use this or that form of handle or frame. It might come to be a point of faith to believe that the drawings were done while the artist was wholly or partially entranced.

On the other hand, some sceptics would assert that the pictures were imaginary, or, at most, founded on mere observations made in the dissecting-room.   More acute observers would see that *something* more than mere invention had been at work, and would suppose that the drawings had been the result of marvellously careful induction, made by comparing the phenomena observed in the dead eye with the symptoms of living patients. At last, in the new civilization, someone living outside the tempest of rival theories, and studying optics for himself, would re-discover the principle of the ophthalmoscope, make one, and actually *see* living retinas.   At once he would perceive that all existing theories alike were provisional working-hypotheses, *i.e.*, mere expressions of ignorance of the essential fact; and that the drawings of the mythical 19th century artists must have been really made by the use of just such an implement as his own.

Now, our discoverer of the future would probably be an aimable man, willing enough to share the joy of his new discovery with whoever desired to possess it; and equally willing to abstain from worrying with it persons who had no such desire.   The mental condition of those who erect working-hypotheses into articles of faith, and who like consecrated theories better than Truth, would be too utterly foreign to his conceptions for him to argue with them.   As for those who should desire both to retain their theories about the old drawings, and also to use the new instrument, he would consider them differentiated from ordinary lunatics only by not possessing the sincerity of the latter.   He would publish an account of his discovery, for the benefit of whoever wished to read about it; and, having done so, would feel he had fulfilled his duty to society; and would not think himself bound to disturb himself any further.

, As some readers may not be acquainted with the nature of the ophthalmoscope, I will tell my parable over again in a simpler form. Suppose there was an island, the inhabitants of which were unacquainted with the principle of numeration, and therefore could only write in numbers singly. They would be able to add and multiply numbers only so far as they could reckon. They would know what such simple numbers as " three times five " make; and very clever and persevering ones might know what twelve times twelve make. But about all large numbers they would have to guess; they would have opinions, and discuss, and generally turn out wrong. If they had a tradition among them that certain ancestors of theirs, called Moses and Isaiah, used to pronounce oracularly as to what numbers " like the trees in a forest for multitude " came to, when multiplied together, and *always turned out right*, they would frame a provisional working-hypothesis that Moses and Isaiah were "inspired," and would argue and jangle as to the precise nature of the " inspiration." Then suppose some islander found out how to " carry," that fortunate individual would know exactly how Moses and Isaiah made sure of their results. And of course the supporters of the rival theories about inspiration would join in calling him hard names; and equally of course he would not mind what they said, but would go on his own way, and wait till events justified his faith in Rational Arithmetic *versus* fanciful guesses.

Now the situation in which the modern discoverers of Mathematical Logic found themselves, was very much like that of our hypothetical new Helmholtz, or the island discoverer of the process of "carrying." Certain ancient Prophets had discovered a means—not of *communicating with the Unseen* (for every man, and woman, and child, and beast does that, until his faculties have been trampled out by the process called nowadays "Education"), but—of making communication with the Unseen *safe*, by applying a mechanical test to ascertain exactly what is being communicated; to distinguish, that is to say, the Inspiration of Truth from the suggestions of the diseased brain. The difference between old Scriptural and merely poetic inspiration consists precisely in the fact that the inspired men of Palestine possessed such a test. The difference between Prophecy and pseudo-prophecy in old times, consisted in applying the test with utter fidelity, in allowing it to act with mechanical accuracy. Babbage, Gratry, and Boole revived that test. They published their books. Then, finding themselves confronted with dishonest folly, they left the world to come to its senses at its leisure.

CHAPTER VI

BABBAGE ON MIRACLE

"If the children of men are silent, iron and stone shall cry out Hosannah."

CHARLES BABBAGE is chiefly known to the world as the inventor of a machine intended to spare the labour of calculating numerical series. In the course of its construction, he had to make a thorough study of the Laws of natural sequence, so far as these are embodied in processes of successive additions. But the man who would think of undertaking such a task at all was sure to see the importance of saturating himself with a further knowledge of Nature's series. He investigated not only those mathematical series the equations of which are known, and which underlie such natural curves as planet-paths, lines of refraction, &c. ; but also those forms of Natural sequence the mathematical expressions of which have not yet been ascertained, such as geologic changes, the development of plants and animals, &c. He had nothing to lose or gain by any conclusion to which he might be led ; he had one all-absorbing end in view, the perfecting of his machine; and, for that object, it mattered nothing what the Laws of Nature should turn out to be ; the one desideratum was that he, Babbage, should know what they were, and embody them truly in the construction of his cogs and wheels. One of the facts which he discovered was this :—For one series (numerical or phenomenal) which goes on uniformly, there are an almost infinite number which either sooner or later have interruptions or Singular Terms. His arguments cannot be fully entered on here ; but the main result is this :—Whoever adduces the inflexibility of Law to prove the improbability of Miracle, only proves that he does not understand the connection between Law and Phenomena. No miracle, Mr. Babbage considers, could be, *à priori*, so improbable as it is that man should learn the true law of any sequence by observing an *uninterrupted* series of phenomena. He says :—"It is more probable that any law, at the knowledge of which we have arrived by observation, shall be subject to one of those violations which, according to Hume's definition,[1] constitute a miracle,

---

[1] Hume had "deduced the *à priori* probability against the occurrence of miracle from universal experience."

than that it should not be so subjected. . . . The class of laws subject to interruption is far more extensive than that of laws which are uninterrupted. It is, in fact, infinitely more numerous. Therefore the probability of any law with which we have become acquainted by observation being part of a much more extensive law, and having, to use mathematical language, *singular points* or *discontinuous functions* contained within it, is very large." "Miracles are not deviations from the laws assigned by the Almighty for the government of matter and of mind. . . . They are the exact fulfilment of much more extensive laws than those we suppose to exist. In fact, if we were endued with acuter senses and higher reasoning faculties, they are the very points we should seek to observe, as the test of any hypothesis we had been led to frame concerning the nature of those laws. Even with our present imperfect faculties we frequently arrive at the highest confirmation of our views of the laws of Nature by tracing their action under *singular* circumstances." "A miracle may be only an exact fulfilment of a general law of Nature, under such singular circumstances that, to those imperfectly acquainted with that law, it appears to be in direct opposition to it." "All miracles are prophecies ; . . . they are revelations, more or less in advance, of events which, although in real accordance, are apparently in direct contradiction to the laws of Nature."

The work from which the above extracts are taken[1] forms probably the best introduction in our language to the art of inductive reasoning. It is simple in style, almost entirely free from technicalities, and very reverent

[1] Ninth Bridgewater Treatise.   Murray.

in tone.   It makes no attacks on the special beliefs of
any sect, but confines itself to neutralizing the poisonous
doctrines of those who oppose Science to Religion, by
showing that all attacks made on Faith in the name of
Science must necessarily rest on a mistaken apprehension
of the bearing of scientific observation.   There are, probably, out of the Scriptures, few sublimer conceptions
than Mr. Babbage's Vision of future rewards and punish-
ments ; he pictures the cruel man, not tortured by an
angry Deity, but mercifully awakened to true self-
knowledge, by being endowed with senses fine enough
to perceive things as God sees them ; and to hear the
reverberations, through the infinite ether-spaces, of the
long-silenced cries of his victims.   It might have been
supposed that the book would immediately take a place
among educational text-books, among which it is well
suited to rank high.   But the education of the country
was, in those days, in the hands of ecclesiastical parties;
and, by common consent, the book was ignored.

The study of Mathematics seems to have a wonderful
tendency both to induce religious faith and to counteract
the influence of dogmatists ; and the instinct of the
latter class seems to detect this without their being able
to give any rational explanation of their dislike.   There
is a mysterious link, more easy to perceive than to
describe, between mathematical truth and the doctrine
of the Fatherhood of God in its old Mosaic sense.   Of
course, the fact of learning at second-hand, and applying
to practical uses results arrived at by the investigations
of others, has no relation to any sort of religion ; it
leaves the field equally clear for dogma or for atheism.
But whoever has truly apprehended the nature of the

process of mathematical discovery, knows henceforth that the mind in him which can go through such a process is the child of the Creator.   Contact with the Mathesis which underlies human thought constitutes an absolute revelation or unveiling of Deity.   For this reason mathematicians are usually disliked by priests ; the true mathematician has (though in a very humble manner and small degree) " seen God " ; and the slightest glimpse of that vision is often sufficient to destroy the possibility of believing in priest-made and partial deities. Mr. Babbage says nothing against any particular doctrine ; but under all his statements there resounds perpetually, as a deep harmonic undertone, the implied thought : " Nature is the representation of the action of those mathematical laws which can also be represented by interrupted numerical series ; I have made a machine which is able to represent to the eye the action of some mathematical laws and the existence of certain interrupted series ; therefore my mind is, in its own little way, akin to the Creative Mind.   I believe that some such events as those called miraculous must have taken place during some portion of the history of our planet ; but my faith in God rests on no testimony concerning such past wonders ; for I stand in presence of the perpetual miracle that man is made in the Image of God ; a sharer in His power to understand numerical law and impose it on matter ; a sharer in His power to apprehend moral law and to be the author of joy and woe : a sharer in His power to trace events to their causes ; and therefore a sharer in His own immortality.   I am, by natural inheritance, a child of the Living God ; and when He has anything to say to me He can say it without the intervention of a priest." The clergy decided that Mr. Babbage was " an unbeliever "; and the then rising generation lost the benefit of his aid, to the great injury of both Religion and Science—" Friends whom we cannot think apart "; but which, thanks to ecclesiastical jealousies, are made to " seem each other's foe." It is impossible not to detect, in the antagonism excited by such work as that of Mr. Babbage, the same feelings which caused some persons in an Irish town to ill-use a sick and inoffensive stranger (who, as it afterwards turned out, was a Jewess); " She says she don't want the parson, nor yet the priest; so she must be *something* queer "—the same spirit which has made Gentiles in all ages taunt Judaism with the question—" Where is thy God ? "

The result of introducing Mr. Babbage's book into a school, is a spontaneous development of the feeling expressed in the Pentateuch: that properly taught people are a nation of priests and can find God each for himself. The book to which he gave the name " Ninth Bridgewater Treatise " can occasionally be procured at second-hand; and whoever reads it carefully finds it the entrance to a rich mine of religious truth, of a peculiarly elastic and liberal kind. Its teaching leaves the mind free to believe without difficulty in the existence of *any* order of phenomena, however miraculous-seeming, for which there may appear to be sufficient evidence; but destroys the inclination to address actual *worship* to anything except the Divine Unity.

CHAPTER VII

GRATRY ON LOGIC

" Blessed are they that have not seen and yet believe."

MATHEMATICAL Logic used to be expressed in Geometric or quasi-Geometric diagrams. We now write it usually in a terminology borrowed from Algebra.

Modern Mathematical Logic may be said to be a tree, whose root is represented by the Newtonian Fluxion-method; and its trunk by the *Logique* of Gratry[1]; while its main branches are such works as those of Babbage, De Morgan, Boole, and Hinton; and the Sciences of Quaternions and of the so-called Fourth-Dimensional Mathematics. Carrying on the same simile, we might add that the numerous little twigs of special methods thrown off from the main boughs would have all the more chance of being fruitful if they were not so ready to sever their connection with the stock from which they sprang. As a matter of chronology, the treatises of Babbage, De Morgan, and Boole were published before the first appearance of the *Logique*. But then it must be remembered that Science is not created by the printer; books merely represent, in visible form, a thought-growth which has its actual existence in the Mind of Humanity; and the chronological order in which the several parts of a new Science are projected on to the surface of Literature is not always identical with the order in which they were evolved. Mathematical Logic will be best understood by those who

[1] *Logique*, Gratry, 2 vols. Douniol, Paris.

master the ideas of Gratry before entering upon the study of the more detailed but less philosophically comprehensive treatises of the other writers referred to above. As a matter of fact, neither Babbage nor Boole could have done what he did had he not perceived the truth of some principle analogous to that of Gratry.

And there is no greater hindrance to human progress than lack of piety towards Humanity's best teachers. The statement may be considered a truism; but unfortunately we are all too prone to neglect truisms. Principles so self-evident that no one disputes them, occupy less attention than do theories about which it is possible to get up a controversy; and the settlement of a fierce dispute is often best effected by insisting on the practical recognition of some principle which everybody concerned is disregarding, precisely because nobody has attempted to deny its truth. I repeat :—

There is no greater hindrance to progress than lack of piety towards great teachers; this is well shown by the whole history of Logic since the publication of Gratry's *Logique* in 1855.

Any Seer of a great comprehensive Truth, such as Gratry, is necessarily ahead of his age. He may be, in a sense, appreciated by his contemporaries; that is to say, he may be loved for his goodness, and admired because of certain secondary results of the intellectual Vision which has been vouchsafed to him; but the very essence of such a man's position is that he is seeing truths for which the world around him is not yet ready. When Gratry was writing his Logic, he was looking *through* the intellectual *débâcle* which was then only beginning, and *beyond* it, to the new-created thought-world which might arise from amid the chaos, if the next generation would wisely consider its ways. No reader can properly understand Gratry who does not realize the nature of the cataclysm of which he was watching the beginning; and few persons in his time had any adequate conception of what was coming on the intellectual world. The condition of confusion which he foresaw in prophetic vision, we know as an indisputable and terrible *fait accompli.* He wrote, therefore, rather for us than for his contemporaries; to them he brought, chiefly, a warning, unintelligible to the majority, of stormy weather ahead; to us he offers practical pilotage through an actual hurricane.

But, alas! how shall we persuade young men trained in " the newest methods," that an Oratorian monk of fifty years ago was a better logician than they? "Gratry? oh! no doubt he was very clever for his time. But— he had not read any of our modern authorities; what can he have known of our new methods?" The young teacher, who is preparing pupils for examinations by the help of the last new text-book, and who perhaps hopes to make a name for himself by compiling a still newer one, resents being told of one greater than the author most in repute. So it happens that the writer, who was hardly understood in his own day because he was so far ahead of the age, is shunted into oblivion, when the time comes when he could be understood, because it suits the purposes of interested persons to believe that he is behind their age. The main cause of the chaotic condition into which our thought-life has fallen, is the feverish impatience of teachers, each of whom wants to make his own voice heard. But any teacher who is weary of the conflict between Science and Religion, between Knowledge and Faith, between the valuable Lessons of Materialism and the consoling belief in the spiritual world; any teacher who sincerely desires, not to make a cheap and noisy fame for himself, but to find Truth and Peace for the young souls committed to his care, might do well to devote a quiet vacation to the study of Gratry's *Logique*.

Our author begins by clearly recognizing that mathematics is not so much a department of human thought as the ground-plan of all sane thought; he treats mathematical Science, not as a special set of truths, but as a map of the country in which Truth is to be found. He of course entirely repudiates the profane notion that mathematical Logic can afford any proof or disproof of religious truths; but he shows that mathematical reasoning throws light on the nature of valid proof of every kind. The faculties by which the existence of God is revealed to us are hyper-intellectual; the processes by which we learn spiritual truth are extra-syllogistic; and it pleases a certain school of reasoners to deny their validity. Gratry shows that, but for the exercise of similar faculties and the use of similar processes, we could have discovered nothing of the Higher Mathematics. It pleases certain Agnostics to assert that "it is impossible to reason from the finite to the Infinite." The same objection was formerly made against the Integral Calculus, but the Integral Calculus is now an accepted fact; and any one who cares to learn can know exactly how to "integrate a finite expression to Infinity," and can make sure that his results are absolutely correct. No true mathematician depends on testimony for his knowledge of mathematics ; each has within himself as absolute a personal conviction of the validity of the processes by which he works out his results, as if those processes were purely syllogistic. None the less is that conviction arrived at by a mode of mental action essentially of the same nature as that far more vigorous and sustained mental exercise by which we arrive at a sound and rational faith in God.

" Reasoning is not one process only, it contains two processes, equally valid ; but the second is by far the most powerful and most fertile. The syllogistic process *deduces*, passing from like to like. It never leaves its original stand-point ; it never rises above that stand-point. It develops what it originally possessed. The other process, the dialectic, rises above its own starting-point ; it does not merely develop the material which it originally possessed, it acquires fresh material. . . . This process passes from the finite to the Infinite. . . . This is the process of prayer. . . .Whence it follows that the human mind is capable of a process which, when it is taught as a part of Logic, will give wings to Logic which before had only feet. . . . The Logic of the highest philosophers, both practical and theoretical, has always had wings. But the class of average thinkers exerts itself chiefly in trying to cut those wings, and seems to have succeeded. They must learn to recognize their error, or rather their crime." The author then quotes the following passage from Cournot :—" The process by which the mind seizes new truths is often quite distinct from that by which it connects known truths together ; and most important truths have been first seen by the help of that *philosophic sense* which precedes rigorous proof." Gratry objects to Cournot speaking as if one process was less *rigorous* than the other. And, in fact, we are quite as sure what is the result of an " integration to Infinity," as of what is the answer to a Rule of Three sum.

Suppose that a marble is running round in an elliptical groove under our eyes. Geometry enables us to investigate the relations between the various portions of the course which we see it pursue. But we know its course by direct inspection. Geometry can but arrange into a convenient form, information which we have gathered by observation; or, at most, it shortens the processes by which we acquire information. But when an Astronomer has observed a small portion of the orbit of a heavenly body, it disappears from his ken. He has to construct in imagination its future path, guided by knowledge of the hidden law of its motion. In order to do so, he must resort to the method of the Infinitesimal Calculus; the method thus described by Gratry :—" We have analyzed the finite in order to know the infinitesimal. From the knowledge given by the study of the finite, we have eliminated the quality of finiteness; what remains is true for the infinitesimal; that is to say, for the analysis and knowledge of the Indivisible and the Infinite. We have analyzed the discontinuous, the divisible, the finite; and have found therein the law of the Continuous, the Indivisible, the Infinitesimal."

But when we know the theoretical law of the planet's course, how do we know that, when we have lost sight of it, it still continues to obey the Laws of Mathematics ? No Syllogistic Logic can prove that it does not wander, lawlessly, into space. Yet the mathematician ventures to construct, in imagination, its whole course. He is enabled to do so by an act of *Faith*—faith in the Great Unity Who governs Nature; faith which is the evidence of things not seen. This act of Faith is so elementary and spontaneous, that only a few deep thinkers have recognized it for what it is. But slight as it is, all the delights and powers conferred by the Higher Mathematics are the reward of that simple trust! See how The Unity keeps His ancient covenant with man! Eye hath not seen, nor ear heard, nor hath it yet entered into the heart of man to conceive, what He hath in store for those that love Him!

And slight as is the act of faith needed to understand transcendental mathematics, many are unable to perform it. There are so-called mathematicians who confess themselves unable to see the validity of the reasoning on which the Higher Mathematics rests; they only see that it must be somehow right because predicted eclipses and comets appear in due season; and they therefore assume the legitimacy of the stand-point whence predictions are made; but their own mental action goes no deeper than working out the syllogistic consequences of a knowledge which they do not properly possess. They believe because they have seen prediction fulfilled. Blessed are they who believe in The Unity before they see. No possession of any fact which we know only through the intellect or the senses can equal the intimate and rapturous sense of Union with the Great Unity which is given to him who is enabled by faith to trace in imagination the exact course of a planet out of sight.

Now if persons incapable of understanding transcendental mathematics should presume to claim from true mathematicians a profession of ignorance about all of which they themselves are ignorant, such arrogance would faintly picture that of much (so-called scientific) Agnosticism.

Gratry seems to have foreseen that the Science of Induction would never be developed except by the unselfish co-operation of several men, each of whom should be willing to subordinate his own personal work to the carrying out of a common aim. Mr. Boole's work was, as he gratefully acknowledged, made possible by the generous and self-forgetting aid freely given to him by many contemporary mathematicians; and in particular by Professor De Morgan, who seemed to take a pleasure in effacing himself to bring forward the man whom he might have been expected to feel a rival. And one of my pleasantest recollections of Mr. Boole himself, is his studying with loving and almost rapturous delight the pages of the Oratorian Father, who had stated with masterly and exhaustive completeness the fundamental principle which he himself had been vainly endeavouring to express.

CHAPTER VIII

GRATRY ON STUDY

" Seek ye the old paths."

IT is not only as showing the true nature of logical evidence that Gratry throws light on the intellectual problems of our day. His treatment of the question— What constitutes valid evidence? contains an answer partial, of course, but certainly sound as far as it goes, to that other question :—What constitutes true *Education* ?

The special point in debate among teachers just now is, whether Education means teaching children truths, or drawing out the faculties by which man discovers Truth for himself.

One of the most terrible facts with which we have to deal in Education, is that on this point all the real thinkers are on one side, and nearly all the practice[1] on the other. Among those who are really thinking about Education, the unanimity is so great as to be monotonous. We have had unequivocal expressions of opinion at the Education Society. Professor Maurice and James Hinton (who by no means agreed in most respects) were both strong on this point :—Education means educing faculty, and does not mean imparting knowledge or instilling opinions. Theorists say—and say very truly—that no amount or kind of practice in remembering and writing out at examinations results arrived at by the investigations made by other people, constitutes any exercise of the faculties by which truth is discovered, or any adequate preparation for solving the practical problems which present themselves in the course of every human life. They maintain that no child is really being educated, except in so far as those faculties are being educed and strengthened, by the use of which Truth is brought to light from amidst a chaos of contradictory-seeming phenomena.

Yet some power mightier than all arguments is preventing these would-be reformers from effecting their

[1] This was written nearly twenty years ago. It is no longer quite true ; but I let it stand.

purpose. The practical men insist on keeping up a routine of teaching things which can be tested by Examination. It is easy to rail at practical men, but they are the drag on our impetuosity. *Magna est veritas et prevalebit.* A doctrine which does *not* prevail is not, yet, quite true. The resistance of practical men to our efforts is the resistance of the calyx to the premature unveiling of the imperfect corolla. Instead of railing against those who oppose us, would it not be better to mature our ideas and make our method complete, and therefore irresistible?

The truth is that, in the desperate struggle on behalf of the principle that *Education* means *educing faculty*, the supporters of that principle are too much losing sight of the vital question :—What faculties is it most important to educe? Where the advocates of Education *versus* Examination get their own way, the result often is that too much mental force is absorbed into a minute and monkey-like inquisitiveness about visible phenomena, and often the production of a skill, more wonderful than useful, in the observation of certain classes of facts to the neglect of all other facts; and in the study of mathematical methods of analysis of principles, to the neglect of vital comprehension of the principles themselves in their bearing on human development.

Gratry is as sure as any Science-teacher of the present day, that Education means educing the faculties by which man discovers Truth for himself. But :—what Truth? And what faculties? The highest object of intellectual culture, according to Gratry, is to educe and fortify the sense by which we perceive *what the Unseen Teacher is saying to us.*

" Do you know whom you are going to have for your Teacher ? God. The time has come when you will put into practice the command of Christ—' Call no man your master on earth ; for One is your Master, even God.' . . . You have heard and said that God is Light and enlightens every man. Do you believe this ? If so, then accept all the consequences of that belief. If you believe that you have within you a Master Who wills to teach you, say to this Master, as you would say it to a man standing in front of you : ' Master, speak to me ; I am listening.'

"But then, after you have said, 'I am listening,' you must listen. This is simple, but of primary importance.

"In order to listen, we must have silence. Now who, I ask, among men—especially among those who consider themselves thinkers—ever secures for himself silence ?

"All day long the student listens to other men's talk; or else, he talks himself; when he is supposed to be alone, he is making books talk to him as fast as his eye can move along the lines of print. . . . His solitude is peopled, besieged, cumbered . . . by useless talkers and by books which are a mere hindrance to thought. . . . Believe me, one who studies thus will learn little or nothing ; just because there is only one Teacher, and this Teacher is within us ; because we must listen before we can hear Him ; and to listen we must have silence."

Nevertheless, Gratry insists that no man is really educated unless he knows, and knows well, the essential principles of all the important Sciences. His list of requirements seem at first sight a formidable one. The cultivated man must know enough of the Higher Mathematics to understand the principles of Mathematical Induction ; because " he who can understand the principle of Induction will be for ever preserved from atheism and materialism." (This implies a far deeper acquaintance with mathematical philosophy than is necessary to become a Senior Wrangler.) As for Astronomy, Gratry thinks the ignorance of the public about so grand a Science very strange. He mentions successively, Physics, Physiology, Geology, Geography, History, and Moral Science; of each of which he requires the cultivated man to know considerably more than a mere smattering. Finally comes Theology. Gratry is tolerant to those who differ from him in opinion ; but he does not understand how it can happen " that every educated man does not know by heart the Articles of the Christian faith.

"If you are Christians these Articles contain the details of your faith. . . . If you are enemies of Christianity, take the trouble to know what are the statements against which you are fighting ; your blows will thus be dealt less at random."

Gratry has here laid bare one of the principal causes of the mental confusion of our time. No man, to whatever denomination he belongs, ought to be considered *educated*, who does not know what are the essential principles both of Mosaic teaching and of the Catholic Faith. What, for instance, does European History mean, to one who has no clear conception of the nature of those thoughts and feelings which have moulded our civilization ?

But the question naturally presents itself :—If we are to spend a large portion of our time in listening to the Voice of the Unseen, instead of reading, how can such a mass of positive information be acquired? Gratry's answer is similar in kind to that given later by Hinton, but expressed in a manner both more methodical and more safe than Hinton's. Gratry bids the student keep perpetually by him, for his guidance, the living belief that, as The Creator is One, so must the Science of that which He has created be one also. " Fear neither the magnitude, nor the number, nor the diversity of the Sciences. Study will be simplified, harmonized and fertilized, by comparing one Science with another." We seem to hear Moses of old proclaiming the formula of freedom and of power:—" Hear, O Israël! The divided gods enslave us; the Deliverer from bondage is the Unity."

And as we might facilitate our work by unifying the Sciences into One Science, so we should also treat the revelations of all times as One Eternal Truth. This is best done by studying each Science according to the historical method; letting the culture of to-day flow into our minds in natural sequence from that of yesterday. It is vain that we rise early and late take rest, and anxiously devour many books; to those who love The Great Unity, He gives knowledge even while they sleep.

If any social phenomenon of our time is more astounding than the ignorance of important facts displayed by many professed scientists, it is the feebleness of mental grasp exhibited by many students of the so-called " mental and moral " Sciences. Their thought-modes suggest nothing so much as the thin rapid pulse generated by exhaustion and over-excitement. This singular psychic condition is clearly traceable to the fatigue caused by the destruction of ancient landmarks. A cultivated mind shrinks indeed from acknowledging as the substance of its *faith* any more of Truth than so much as it has made its own ; but the limit of personal faith is not necessarily that of historical knowledge. Unity of thought is promoted, and the process of self-culture enormously facilitated, by having always at hand in one's memory, in a compact form, the best results of the mental labour of preceding ages. A creed or formulary acts as what Hinton called "an unconscious constant" ; a crystallizing thread round which atoms of knowledge may gradually gather, instead of being swept away by every current of thought, or retained only by vehement effort. Nothing makes study at once so exhausting and so unprofitable as the absence of any frame-work of registered propositions. Nothing, therefore, can be more fatal to intellectual progress than the random destruction of those ancient formulæ which create, as it were, a common language between men ; and between the successive epochs of life, both personal and national. The attempt to acquire power and freedom for intellectual pursuits by keeping oneself *ignorant* of ancestral Theology would seem to be about on a level, for practical efficacy, with the attempt to gain facilities for the study of human life by living like a savage. Even those who wish to explore barbarous regions find that they can do so to more purpose if they carry about with them, in a compact form, a judicious selection of civilized appliances. Setting aside all considerations of religion, the European who is not familiar with the various clauses of the Athanasian Creed gives one the same sense of *lack of culture* as does an Englishman unacquainted with Shakspere, or a Jew who has not read Isaiah.

And the vicious system which is sweeping away the frame-work of association by which we are connected with the past, is only consistent in its folly, in that it provides no substitute whereby the individual child may be connected with its own past. As soon as a child has passed an Examination in a certain "standard," he casts aside that standard, and learns something different. There is no formula which is solemnly repeated every day or every week throughout his school career. Suicidal blindness could no further go.

We may sum up the reflections suggested by the *Logique* of Gratry, by saying that the feverish feebleness of ephemeral Scientism is a part of that grand process of Natural Selection by which irreverence, impiety, and conceit are, in each age, weeded out, to leave room for something more worthy to endure. Excessive specialization is always more or less *idolatrous*. Those who alternate an intelligent interest in the Science of their own day with seasons of pious meditation on the aspirations of the mighty dead, renew their strength like young eagles, and their days shall be long in the land. They shall inherit the possessions of time-serving idolaters. They shall attract peoples that they know not, and nations who knew them not shall seek them ; and great shall be the peace of their children ; for such is the heritage of the servants of the Lord.

CHAPTER IX

BOOLE AND THE LAWS OF THOUGHT

"Hear, O Israel, the Lord our God is Unity."

SIXTY years ago, logicians had concluded that it would be convenient to express ordinary statements about facts in some sort of Arithmetical or Algebraic notation, so as to be able to work out the logical consequences of premises with the same ease as we work sums. Many attempts were made to create such a notation; but none of them proved satisfactory. There was in Lincoln a school-master in humble circumstances, who had, when a mere lad, solved for himself a problem of a very different order. It had occurred to him that the Scripture writers must have had some reason for laying so much stress on the command never to think of *The Great All* except as a *Unity*. He had acquired the habit of thinking of each class of things as a fraction of Unity. He found that this habit simplified all study; and by strict adherence to it he had, in the very small amount of leisure at his disposal, made of himself a fairly good linguist, a learned metaphysician, and a mathematician distinguished for the originality and vigour of his methods of investigation. When, therefore, he realized what was the problem over which logicians were pondering, it naturally occurred to him to try on their behalf the experiment of using the Arithmetical Symbol of *Unity* for *Universe of Thought*. Immediately the notation fell easily into order, and all the difficulties vanished.

As simple obedience to the commands of the Pentateuch had enabled George Boole to solve the questions
which the logicians of the 19th century could not solve,
it seemed probable that the writers of Scripture knew
more than was commonly supposed about the normal
action of the human mind.   He set himself the task of
making a serious study of the Laws of Thought-sequence;
aided by the conversation of a Jewish friend, a teacher
of Hebrew at Lincoln.   In 1854 he published a book to
which he gave the title, *The Laws of Thought.*

A strange result ensued.   The author had felt obliged
to show that his system was not a mere fanciful outcome
of religious fervour; and, in order to do this, he had
interspersed his serious analysis with exhibitions of
delicate and skilful modes of extracting the legitimate
consequences from masses of premises.   Those who were
on the look-out for *a rapid method of manipulating
syllogisms*, were at first delighted to find their problem
solved ; and it is impossible to speak too highly of the
generosity with which several eminent logicians did
honour to the man of whom they evidently thought only
as a rival in their own line.   But it seems never to have
occurred to them that any one could care for Logic
except as a *method of reasoning*.   They proceeded to
improve the method of the book called *Laws of Thought*,
by leaving out of it all that could throw light on the
Laws of Thought-Sequence !

Mr. Stanley Jevons earned a wide-spread fame as the
improver of Boole's method.   George Boole's own version of the matter was that Mr. Jevons and he were
working for totally different objects, and that no intercourse between them could be of the least use to either.

His chief anxiety seemed to be to make it impossible that Mr. Jevons should appear as in any way authorized by him. In later years Mr. Jevons was heard to say: "Boole means something that no one has understood yet; the world is not ready to understand him." The solution of Mr. Jevons' perplexity might have been found in the very title of the work on which he was commenting. The symbols which such logicians as he quite rightly discard from Boole's notation, because they are useless and cumbersome and even misleading when employed to work out logical problems, are the necessary implements which those must learn to use who wish to apply mathematical processes to analyze for themselves the Laws of Thought. Had George Boole been chiefly aiming to supply logicians with a ready-made method, his method must be confessed a very bad one; he was aiming to set the example of studying the Laws of Mental Action.

The nature of the change introduced by George Boole into logical analysis may be summed up thus:—In working a sum or equation, we seem to ourselves to be only manipulating and transforming the particular statements contained in the so-called "stating" of our question. But these very transformations are effected by means of our knowledge of certain general truths about number, such, for instance, as those registered in the multiplication-table. "Working" a sum means combining its special statements with general statements which are latent in the mind. Working a thought-sum, then, should mean transforming its premises by combining them with our general knowledge of the Laws of Mental Action. And, in fact, the Aristotelian syllogism was, so far as it went, a process of this very kind; it brought a certain thought-law into contact with the special premises of each argument; and, by means of that general law, extracted the conclusion. To make Logic a more powerful instrument than it had hitherto been, what was needed was not, as Gratry seems to suggest, to import into it a new process, the process of faith; but to extend and make freer and more vigorous our use of that process; seeing that every syllogism is, so far as it goes, an act of faith in the general Laws of the Creative Logos. The Aristotelian Logic was, in fact, an Arithmetic of reasoning, analogous to such an Arithmetic of number as might be evolved by a race whose general knowledge of the Laws of Number amounted to familiarity with the "twice" column of the multiplication-table.

We may say then that what logicians had been seeking, though without quite knowing what they sought, was a Logic made wide and vigorous by using all attainable knowledge of the Laws of Thought as freely as, in working sums, we use our knowledge of the Laws of Number. Such a Logic, it need hardly be added, is yet to be created; though George Boole did a little towards laying its foundations. He brought to light three great principles of mental action :—

First, that all sound thinking treats the Universe of Thought as a Unity; and classes of things as fractions of Unity; and that Unity itself as a fraction of a larger Unity.

Secondly, that we cannot deal logically with any statement except by comparing it impartially with the opposite statement.

Thirdly, that sound Thought is always essentially a free Pulsation between extremes. All selection, whether by an adult for himself, or by a teacher for his pupils, should consist in selection of the question to be studied. When once we have decided what we will think about, we must think with perfect impartiality on both sides. In mathematical language we state this by saying that every sound thought-process which can be carried on with respect to any element (x), depends in some way or other on considering x, first as *Unity* (*i.e.* Universal and absolute throughout the Universe of Thought), and then as *Zero* (*i.e.* non-existent in the Universe of Thought), and then combining the two conceptions. Right conduct (it is often said) is that which keeps the mean between two extremes. Now to know the mean we must know the extremes. Sound thought is related to correct conduct as the pulsation of a Light-ray is related to the onward path of the ray. Whatever hampers the free, side-ways pulsation of the wave from one extreme to the other, interferes with the pure whiteness of the Light; whatever hampers the free swinging of the mind between extremes of opinion, obstructs man's vision of what is right in moral conduct.

A country watchmaker, being asked why being dirty made a watch go fast instead of slow (as the questioner would have expected), replied: "Well, you see, when the wheels are clogged with dirt, it *don't* go; not to say *go;* it only niggles-like." This is the explanation of the hurry and fever of life. Our minds are clogged with prejudices and trammelled with superstitions; and they don't really work, they "only niggle-like." We think we are giving our children freedom by presenting to them a mass of novel ideas, the truth of which has not yet been tested, and by indoctrinating them with a mass of prejudices which differ from those of our forefathers chiefly by being expressed in new phraseology; it would be better to present to them a few subjects of study, selected according to some order which has been tested by long experience; and, when once a child's attention has been called to any topic, encourage him to think of it with absolute freedom and utter impartiality. This, and not any particular method for manipulating masses of syllogisms, is the main outcome of Boole's mathematical analysis of the Laws of Thought. It is a curious compilation; over-weighted with too great a mass and variety of material. In its attempt to bring the intellect and heart to work in unison, it fails to make its appeal to either easily intelligible. It needs a far closer study than ordinary readers can be expected to give to an author. Nevertheless, it is a very amusing book, because of its latent satire on those mental processes which religious and ethical writers call "thinking." A few quotations will make clear the author's opinion of ordinary religious controversy.

" I shall examine what are the actual premises involved ; whether those premises be expressed or implied. By the actual premises I mean whatever propositions are assumed in the course of the argument, without being proved, and are employed as parts of the foundation upon which the final conclusion is built. . . . The chief practical difficulty of this inquiry will consist, not in the application of the method to the premises once determined, but in ascertaining what the premises are. In what are regarded as the most rigorous examples of reasoning applied to metaphysical questions, it will occasionally be found that different trains of thought are blended together; that particular but essential parts of the demonstration are given parenthetically, or out of the main course of the argument; that the meaning of a premise may be in some degree ambiguous; and, not unfrequently, that arguments, viewed by the strict laws of formal reasoning, are incorrect or inconclusive. The difficulty of determining and distinctly exhibiting the true premises of a demonstration" (in a book which we are studying and analyzing), "may, in such cases, be very considerable. But it is a difficulty which must be overcome by all who would ascertain whether a particular conclusion is proved or not, whatever form they may be prepared or disposed to give to the ulterior process of reasoning. It is a difficulty, therefore, which is not peculiar to the method of" mathematical analysis, "though it manifests itself more distinctly in connection with this method than with any other. So intimate, indeed, is this connection, that it is impossible, employing the method of this treatise, to form even a conjecture as to the validity of a conclusion, without a distinct apprehension and exact statement of all the premises upon which it rests. In the more usual course of procedure" (i. e. verbal analysis), "nothing is, however, more common than to examine some of the steps of a train of argument, and thence to form a vague general impression of the scope of the whole, without any such preliminary and thorough analysis of the premises which it involves.

"The necessity of a rigorous determination of the real premises of a demonstration ought not to be

regarded as an evil; especially as, when that task is ac-
complished, every source of doubt or ambiguity is
removed.   In employing the method of this treatise . . .
the process of inference is conducted with a precision
which might almost be termed mechanical."—*Laws of
Thought*, ch. xiii. §§ 1, 2.

" There are many special departments of science which
cannot be completely surveyed from within, but require
to be studied also from an external point of view, and
to be regarded in connection with other and kindred
subjects, in order that their full proportions may be understood." (*Laws of Thought*, ch. viii. § 1).   The above
passage is in line with George Boole's opinion that no
Church can properly be reformed from within.   The
errors of a Church, he considered, must always be
attacked from without.   The ideal condition, of course,
would be that Reformers within a Church should
voluntarily seek the assistance of those who look on from
the outside; but George Boole could not be induced to
believe that such liberality was possible.

The following passage is interesting, as bearing on the
question of the relation between rival systems of Theology.

" If the general truths of Logic are of such a natute
that when presented to the mind they at once command
assent, wherein consists the difficulty of constructing the
Science of Logic?   Not in collecting the materials of
knowledge, but in discriminating their nature, and
determining their mutual place and relation.   All sciences
consist of general truths: but of those truths, some only
are primary and fundamental, others are secondary and
derived.   The laws of elliptic motion, discovered by
Kepler, are general truths in Astronomy, but they are

not its fundamental truths. And it is so in the purely mathematical sciences. An almost boundless diversity of theorems which are known, and an infinite possibility of others as yet unknown, rest together upon the foundation of a few simple axioms; and yet these are all *general* truths. They are truths which, to an intelligence sufficiently refined, would shine forth in their own unborrowed light, without the need of those connecting links of thought, those steps of wearisome and often painful deduction, by which the knowledge of them is actually acquired. Let us define as fundamental those laws and principles from which all other general truths of science may be deduced, and into which they may all be again resolved. Shall we then err in regarding that as the true Science of Logic which, laying down certain elementary laws, confirmed by the very testimony of the mind, permits us thence to deduce, by uniform processes, the entire chain of its secondary consequences, and furnishes, for its practical applications, methods of perfect generality? Let it be considered whether in any science, viewed either as a system of truth or as the foundation of a practical art, there can properly be any other test of the completeness and the fundamental character of its laws, than the completeness of its system of derived truths, and the generality of the methods which it serves to establish. Other questions may indeed present themselves. Convenience, prescription, individual preference, may urge their claims and deserve attention. But as respects the question of what constitutes Science in its abstract integrity, I apprehend that no other considerations than the above are properly of any value."—*Laws of Thought*, ch. i § 5.

It is interesting to notice that the life-law of the brain, taught by Gratry, can be illustrated by means of a plain forked stick. But in order to teach geometrically Boole's complicated method of critical analysis, we must also employ the spiral wire or snake-coil. If the writer of the third Chapter of Genesis lived in our prosaic age, he would perhaps formulate his caution thus:—" Study Gratry freely. But beware of allowing yourself to be tempted by Boole's subtle and fascinating method ; or it will surely lead you into mischief."

If he were in a specially honest frame of mind, he might add :—" Because Boole's method may enable you to grasp ideas quite beyond the comprehension of your Rabbi (Don, Pedagogue, or Pope, as the case may be); and therefore necessarily wicked."

CHAPTER X

SINGULAR SOLUTIONS

" I have made out what puts the whole subject of Singular Solutions into a state of Unity."

ALL metaphysicians have known of the existence of a law of antithesis or contradiction in Thought. "We form the conception of man by contrast with that of not-man; we know good by seeing it against a background of evil; the child learns to realize its own personality by coming in contact with things that are not itself." All this is the commonplace of metaphysics. But modern mathematics is leading to the perception that we need something more definite than to see x

against a vague background of *not-x;* we need the special and definite antithetic conception to x within the particular " Universe of Thought " to which x properly belongs. And often we have to investigate a class of things as forming a part of more than one Universe of Thought, and contrast it with not-x in each. As, for instance, we may clear up our conception of " black sheep " by contrasting it, first, with " sheep that are not black " ; secondly, with " black objects that are not sheep "; and so on. The Differential Calculus, however, shows that the mind is feeling after even a more definite mode of contrast than that indicated above. We cannot truly know the Law which governs an organic group of phenomena, unless we allow ourselves to conceive the idea of a Singular Solution of that Law, *i.e.*, an individual which is *constant in some relations as to which the other individuals are variable, and variable in some relations as to which the others are constant.*

Now the so-called Messianic Seers are persons in whom is developed to a high degree the tendency to study ordinary human beings by the method of contrast with an Ideal Man, a sort of Singular Solution of Humanity; of whom they speak as constant in those relations to the Unseen in which we are variable, and fluent in those relations to the visible as to which each of us has his fixed prejudices. This Ideal Man, they assert, is the indispensable Mediator between them and any true knowledge of Humanity. When they have jumped to the conclusion that their need of *conceiving* an Ideal Man is any proof of the actual existence of such an Ideal, visible or Invisible, they err, of course. But, nevertheless, these Messianic Seers are neither dreamers nor maniacs; they are revealing, in the domain of emotion, a Law which the mathematical doctrine of Singular Solutions reveals to the intellect, viz. that the process of conceiving an antithetical exception is a necessary medium between the mind of man and any very thorough comprehension of the Laws which govern Humanity.

The study of the phenomenon of the Messianic Seer-hood became the absorbing interest of George Boole's later years. The chapter on Singular Solutions in his text-book of Differential Equations contains much genuine metaphysical truth expressed in mathematical terminology. He made a special study of the sermons of the strange preacher, F. D. Maurice; and in the last year of his life wrote: " I have made out what puts the whole subject of Singular Solutions into a state of Unity." What strange pulsation of thought must have thrilled from the mind of the great Seer of Messianic Singular Solution, into that of the logician of the Unity, before those words were written, who can guess? The MS. on which George Boole was engaged at the time lies undeciphered in the archives of the Royal Society; no mere mathematician can understand it: and no theologian cares to try. Perhaps it may be deciphered yet; when further progress has been made in knowledge of the correspondence between the normal action of the human mind and its automatic expression by means of notations.

CHAPTER XI

"The Evidence of Things not seen."

MUCH of the tragedy of religious conflict is due to lack of comprehension of the process of *Algebraization.*

I have pointed out how a question which seemed, on its own level, hopelessly unsolvable, is often solved at once by reference to an order of considerations higher than that involved in the question itself. This is especially the case when a *Law of Thought* is appealed to, to settle a discussion about *things.* Laws of things we cannot be said really to know, except in a fumbling and empirical manner; when we have true knowledge, it is because we have discovered the Law of Thought which presided at the Genesis of the Things. I wish to speak in all humility and reverence; but I cannot say less than I mean. We get clues, suggestions of Laws of Thought, by studying things; but whenever we truly *know*, what we know is a Law of Thought, which we have arrived at by discharging from our observation of particular finite things all that made them finite and particular. The elementary geometrician who first conceived the idea of the circle caught his suggestion from looking at things whose forms were approximately round; but, as soon as he had discovered the law of roundness within his own mind, he was able to express roundness in a new material, to state it generally (by scratching it on the sand) in a manner which afforded no clue to the objects from which the suggestion had come to him. And the law of circularity, thus formulated, was henceforth master within him, and governed his appreciation of things. He did not test his Ideal circle by comparing it with the sun or with an apple; on the contrary, he tested the circularity of a fruit by comparing it with his abstract or Ideal circle. His circle then was an *algebraization* of the round outline of the sun or moon, or of a fruit.

In the same way we discover a law of number, first, by thinking of some particular numbers; but as soon as we know the Law, we can state it *Algebraically, i.e.*, in a manner which conveys no information as to what were the particular numbers of which we happened to be thinking when we discovered it. The particular numbers suggested the law to our consciousness; they do not prove it to our reason. When once it has been suggested, it carries its own evidence, independently of particular numbers. And as soon as we have formulated a Law thus algebraically, it is henceforth master within us. Particular statements about number are referred to it; and our opinion as to the truth of those statements is controlled by it. For instance, the law that one number multiplied by a second always comes to the same result as is obtained by multiplying the second by the first was of course suggested to the consciousness first by the observation of some particular pairs of numbers; but it is not proved by reference to any special numbers; it is general and algebraic. And no student thoroughly understands it as a law of number until he understands it in its algebraic statement: $ab = ba$. As soon as he understands the algebraic statement, it becomes master of his thought.

A similar process has been going on throughout the history of religion. For instance, the idea of God as Father *suggested* itself first in connection with the love of animals or men for their progeny. But the latter contains no *proof* of the former. The idea is suggested to the consciousness by particular facts; but those who understand it at all, accept it on its own evidence; and for them it henceforth governs their ideas of particular facts.

Superstition has always been trying to cumber our ideas about God with the pomposity, or vengefulness, or jealousy, or whatever vice happened to prevail in the parents of the particular era. Philosophy has always been trying to *algebraize* our conception of Fatherhood; to present the normal or Ideal Father; and to induce human fathers to conform their conduct to this Ideal.

The difference between our imperfect and fumbling knowledge of things, and our absolute and perfect knowledge about Laws of Thought, has been thus described :—

" The general Laws of Nature are not, for the most part, immediate objects of perception. They are either inductive inferences from a large body of facts,[1] the common truth in which they express, or, in their origin at least, physical hypotheses of a causal nature, serving to explain phenomena and to predict new combinations of them. They are in all cases, and in the strictest sense of the term, *probable* conclusions; approaching, indeed, ever and ever nearer to certainty, as they receive more and more of the confirmation of experience; but of the character of probability, in the strict and proper sense of that term, they are never wholly divested. On

[1] The author means " our mode of stating them are."

the other hand, the knowledge of the laws of mind does not require as its basis any extensive collection of observations.   The general truth is seen in the particular instance, and it is not confirmed by the repetition of instances.   That formula of reasoning which is called the *dictum* of Aristotle *de omni et nullo* expresses a general truth in Logic ; now that truth is made manifest in all its generality by reflection upon a single instance of its application.   And this is both an evidence that the particular principle or formula in question is founded upon some general law or laws of the mind, and an illustration of the doctrine that the perception of such general truths is not derived from an induction from many instances, but is involved in the clear apprehension of a single instance.   In connection with this truth is seen the not less important one that our knowledge of the laws upon which the science of the intellectual powers rests, whatever may be its extent or its deficiency, is not probable knowledge.   For we not only see in the particular example the general truth, but we see it as a certain truth,—a truth our confidence in which will not continue to increase with increasing experience of its verifications. . . . Shall we then err in regarding that as the true science of Logic which, laying down certain elementary laws, confirmed by the very testimony of the mind, permits us then to deduce, by uniform processes, the entire chain of its secondary consequences, and furnishes, for its practical applications, methods of perfect generality ? " [1]

The author has omitted to notice one fact which, from his point of view, probably seemed too self-evident

[1] Boole, *Laws of Thought*, ch. i. §§ 4, 5.

to be worth mentioning, but the ignoring of which causes much confusion in Science; viz. that whereas he who is teaching a Law of things must illustrate his remarks by reference to actual facts, or his whole argument falls to the ground, a principle of Algebraization can just as well be illustrated by reference to imaginary as to real occurrences. When the law of circularity has once been suggested to the mind, it matters nothing whether the object which suggested it was a real or a painted fruit; nor does it matter how nearly it approximated to the circular form. In the same way, the spiral law of thought-progress is equally well illustrated by the narrative of Abraham, whether it be a narration of actual facts or an imaginary tale.

The kind of confusion which is caused in literature by this principle not being understood, will be described in a future Chapter.

There was a time when even mathematical algebraization was considered impious and dangerous. We have grown accustomed to it now. But the algebraizers of the moral world are still the objects of the hatred of other classes of men (and that is by no means the worst part of their destiny, as we shall presently see). Ordinarily a tolerably strong antagonism is kept up between three classes: the supporters of convention, who desire to make some sort of practical life possible, and who object to whatever disturbs popular ideas; the so-called Free-thinkers, who refuse to acknowledge the validity of convention, and who do not believe in the possibility of knowing the true Law of any human relation; the Idealists, who create an ideal moral code according to some standard agreeable to their feelings.

These three classes, in ordinary times, hate each other
with very sufficient cordiality.   There is a fourth class
—honest cautious men who have picked up their notions
of Logic from the study of what is called " Natural
Science," and who imagine that no Law can be truly known
unless it be generalized from a large number of instances.
The Algebraizer is a mark for the sneers of all four
classes.   To the conventional he seems to be defying
Law, because he ignores rules made in ignorance of the
the true Law.   To the self-styled Free-thinkers he seems
to be attacking freedom, because he asserts that there
is a Law which cannot be broken, and which will avenge
attempts to ignore it.   To Idealists he seems to be ex-
tinguishing Light, because their fancy-lamps fade when
he dazzles them by opening the shutters and revealing
the Sun.   And the so-called " scientific " despise him as
rash, because he illustrates his meaning by reference to
only one or two instances, which (as matters of
historical fact) may be of doubtful authenticity.   He
can never do right.   If he speaks, he is arrogant, in that
he professes to know more than other men ; if he keeps
silence, he is contemptuous and proud.   He longs to give
freely that wonder of joy which has been freely given to
him.   He longs to give freely, but Humanity will not
have his gift; yet it reproaches him for hardness, in
that he takes no trouble to slake its thirst for the living
Truth.   If he be of philosophic temperament, he retires
into his study, and confides to his wife, or perhaps to
some favourite dog or cat, refined satires about the
absurd inconsistency of mankind.   But if he be tender-
hearted, his heart breaks, and he dies in despair.   O !
Jerusalem, that stonest the Prophets !

It may be, however, that he loves the Unseen Revealer more than either abstract Science or concrete Humanity. If so, he is preserved from both cynicism and despair. He possesses his soul in patience until it pleases God to make him understood.

In any case, the worst of his doom is still to come. After his death some follower distorts his meaning, so as to make it palatable to the unthinking masses; and uses his name to trample out truth revealed to his successors. An algebraizer of our own day used often to say: " One would accept being crucified; it does not last long; but to have one's words made into an excuse for trampling down the truth revealed through other Seers, that is a doom to make the stoutest heart quail." Of this awful torture Jesus has had eighteen centuries already; and Moses thirty-three. O! Jerusalem, that buildest the tombs of the Prophets, saying: " If we had lived in our fathers' days, we would not have partaken of their crimes."

CHAPTER XII

DEGENERATIONS TOWARDS LUNACY AND CRIME

"We feel as our ancestors thought, and think as our descendants will feel."—J. JACOBS.

IN former Chapters I pointed out the manner in which idleness and superstition fasten on successive revelations; how they in each age make a concrete system of opinion out of what was, in its origin, merely the garment worn by the Pulsation-doctrine in the mind of some Seer. But besides such degraded remains of what once were

truths as are retained in the conscious memory of men
and believed in as doctrines or moral codes, our very
nervous systems have their own unconscious memory,
and preserve idolatries and superstitions which have
died out of the conscious memory.   These are constantly
tending to revert into consciousness.   A good social
system provides for periodic and harmless fits of atavism.
Those are wise who, in holidays, throw off the social
trammels of their own age and revert to an older mode
of existence.   If we live too constantly in the one thin
stratum of convention which we call " present custom,"
we grow weary ; the energy relaxes in spite of us ; and
then at last we fall *involuntarily* into some stratum of
the past.

Books on Lunacy attribute mental disease to physical
causes, which produce weakness of brain-tissue.   It is
quite true that, given an abnormal strain, the stronger
tissues resist it most successfully.   But why should we
put *continuous* strain upon ourselves, such continuity of
strain being contrary to Nature?   It is the nature of
man to stand on his feet, not crawling ; and to exert his
mind to live in the present, not yielding to mere instinct.
But it is also his nature both to return periodically to
the physical position of the earth-worms, and to revert
occasionally to the mental position of the savage.   We
do not wait to lie down till we have fallen from fatigue;
we accustom ourselves and our children to relax and
revert at regular intervals.   Only the exceptionally weak
take such indulgences as lying down during the day ;
but mentally and morally we act as if only the exceptionally weak need lie down at all !

Could I give to each reader the fearful experience

which is gained by occasionally residing, for even a week
or two, in a mad-house, I need not plead in words; but
as that is impossible, I must go on with my appeal to
reason and conscience.

Perhaps nothing in the conduct of our life is so
irrational as our attitude towards the whole subject of
insanity. Because the tendency to yield to certain
sensations *in a spasmodic and irregular way* is a proof
of mental weakness, it is inferred that those sensations
should be discouraged and trampled out by every device
in our power; and that, when they occur, they should
not be heeded. The consequence is, that when they
occur they are often not confessed till too late; and the
secret remains an extra burden on the over-taxed mind.
It would be as rational to suppose that, because tumb-
ling about in the street is a proof of ill-health, therefore
we should neither go to bed at proper times, nor
acknowledge ourselves weary, nor thank God for the gift
of repose. Those very nervous sensations, the yielding
to which in an irregular manner constitutes insanity,
are in reality the alphabet of a system of telegraphy by
which the past is striving to hold converse with us; they
are the solicitations of some lost knowledge urging us
to re-admit it to the mind of the race that was once its
earthly Temple. "Behold, I stand at the door and
knock," says Truth; if the visitor is ignored, his impor-
tunities may drive us mad indeed; the best way to quiet
them is to admit him quietly, and hear what he has to
say. Education should assist us to do this. Many
teachers, however, aim at trampling out our power to
do it. In so far as they are successful, they only retard
progress. Nature, however, always provides a certain

minority of neurotic sensitives, in whom latent ancestral instinct is too strong to be driven out ; it reverts in spite of all the attempts of teachers to suppress it, and drives the subject mad. "The majority call the minority mad," said one wise man ; but it would be far truer to say that the majority drive the minority mad by attempting to suppress truth.

Many unexplained freaks of reversion become intelligible when we remember that any sight or sound which was associated in the ancestry with certain emotions tends to revive those emotions in sensitive descendants. To this fact we give the name of "instinct." The cat who has never before seen a dog, and the dog who has never before seen a cat, get what in a man we should call "a fit of homicidal mania" at sight of each other; an irrational desire to kill each other; because their ancestors had reasons, founded on knowledge and experience, for desiring each other's death. The young beetle who sees for the first time the petal-veining which is to be his honey-guide, no doubt feels throughout his frame the thrill of prophecy of a joy as yet unknown. He follows the guidance which he cannot understand, till he finds the explanation in a new world of delight. "For beast and bird have seen and heard that which man knoweth not;" because man considers his own instincts fit for nothing better than to be brutally trampled underfoot. Therefore, where a beetle becomes harmlessly drunk with joy, a man goes mad of suffering.

A dog and cat can be made devoted friends; not, however, by *ignoring* ancestral instinct, but by studying and guiding it.

Another fruitful source of insanity is the irreverence of teachers' for the process of Algebraization. Most children have more or less of that luminous transparency which enables the individual to perceive Laws of Thought reflected in the workings of his own soul. As was pointed out in a former Chapter, he who has thus perceived a Law of Thought may be (and often is) absolutely sure that he has seen a general Truth. Teachers, forgetting to discriminate between Laws of Thought and Laws of Things, assert that the individual is no standard for the community; and that *no* Law of Nature can be generalized from a single instance. Many intelligent young people are thus made ashamed of the divinest gift within them, the power of spontaneous perception of thought-laws; and destroy the faculty by not using it. In some, however, the tendency to Algebraization is too strong to be repressed. The lad or girl, being told that "common sense and logic oppose themselves to the practice of generalizing from a single instance," draws the conclusion that his teachers are the opponents of what he feels to be the most sacred portion of his mental life; therefore he sets up a course of life openly defiant of "common sense" as embodied in the advice of those around him. For some years he is only "eccentric" and perhaps "unmanageable"; but the strain is often too great for the brain to bear; he has never been taught to distinguish Laws of Thought from Laws of Things; he carries the practice of *generalizing from one instance* over into the domain of things; he reasons from analogy, or jumps to conclusions from mere association of ideas; and falls into a hopeless tangle of delusions;—victim to the wilful irreverence of his

F

teachers, and his own fidelity to the great truths which they are trampling underfoot.

The key-note of the Science of Lunacy is struck in certain organizations which a physician once described to me as "the physical temperament of insanity with a brain impossible to overset." To Abraham, for instance, came weird impulses of reversion to savage customs and a nomad life. In a weak man without faith these would have developed into savagery and homicidal mania. A resolute personal will would have trampled them out, and by doing so injured both intellectual and moral development. But Abraham knew them for what they were—*revelations* of the Unity Who is guiding Humanity. He followed them in cautious reverence; and was led by them, not towards uselessness or crime, but into higher truth. No action becomes absolutely sinful except in so far as it is the result of lack of faith in the Unity. Abraham discovered that sympathetic comprehension of the savagery of the past leads, up the spiral of ascent, towards comprehension of the future destinies of Man. He did not kill his son; he made of him the Founder of a Race.[1]

In the next Chapter, I shall point out how use may be made of nervous disorder (where it unfortunately exists) for the development of Art. But a great deal of insanity and crime might be prevented if the custom prevailed of periodically casting off the conventions of civilization, and reverently reverting to the piety of our savage forefathers, who sought religious Truth direct from Nature, and found it without scholastic and literary appliances. Till we do this, we shall surely find madness an inevitable feature of civilization.

[1] See Appendix.

Now a mad individual can be locked up and forgotten. Occasionally, however, an impulse of atavism seizes on a whole mass of people; too many to be either locked up or ignored. Such a mass, ignorant of ancestral history, and, therefore, not knowing to what their own sensations point, start some weird fantastic movement, related to some portion of ancestral history much as a dream is related to the past experience of the dreamer. Such movements are produced by some stratum of the ancestral past forcing itself into the consciousness of an irreverent and forgetful posterity. A nation lives long in the land which is careful to study its past; partly because such a Nation reverences the spontaneous Revelations of heredity; and does not allow priests and school-masters to trample out its instincts; and, therefore, does not go mad of atavism repressed till it becomes phrensy.

CHAPTER XIII

THE REDEMPTION OF EVIL

"The Bow shall be a Token."

A TRIFLING but interesting confirmation of the Pulsation-doctrine is to be found in a singular fact connected with Art-Needlework.

Nervous disorder, at least in its beginnings, has polar or antithetic phases. A fit of excitement is followed by one of depression, etc. These aberrant moods affect, in some degree, the colour-sense. Let any patient, who has a sensitive retina but no knowledge of Art, try the following experiment:—

Collect a mass of scraps of silks and ribbon, and a bundle of embroidery-silks or wools, of as many shades as possible. (Any soiled or faded remnants of skeins will answer). In the excited mood, tack scraps of ribbon, etc., quite at random, on to some soft foundation (such as a bit of soft woollen or cotton stuff). Choose always whatever colour pleases the eye at the moment,

A few days later, when the mood has changed, the patient should look at her work. The colouring will probably appear, even to herself, hideously crude and coarse. Then begin to embroider upon it, choosing whatever colour pleases the eye. Before selecting a needleful, fix the eyes for a few moments on the spot which seems most crude; then, suddenly, look into the heap of silks and take whatever colour is found most refreshing, embroidering over the selected spot freely and at random. Before threading the needle again, fix the eyes on whatever spot now seems crudest, and choose a needleful while the eye is annoyed from gazing at that one, and so on. Continue to embroider, in any stitches that suit the hand, in all various moods and in different phases of health, till the whole has been brought to a condition in which it does not offend the eye in any mood.

Experts in needlework, when they see work produced under these conditions, say that it has (however rough in execution) the peculiar stamp of colouring which distinguishes *old* Eastern embroideries from all modern imitations, whether Eastern or European, even the most skilful.

After a time, the worker acquires the power to produce at will this peculiar colouring; and can produce it in normal health, and apply it to work containing some principle of design. But, so far as I have discovered, no one seems able to acquire it except by working, at first, at random; and either during illness, or when worried or fatigued. No one can possibly acquire it except by keeping the first few attempts by her for a long time, and working patiently and repeatedly over the same ground. The acquring of skill is much facilitated by the following method.

During the first crude colouring, think freely and strongly of exciting subjects. (This would be dangerous, but for the correction to be presently indicated.) Think of some exciting topic before choosing a colour; and, while using that colour, try to register on the memory, in connection with that particular silk, the thoughts present during its selection. When looking at a crude spot for the purpose of correction, recall the thoughts registered on it; and, before choosing the silk to correct with, try to formulate what some person, who totally disagrees with the worker, would say on the special point associated with that spot.

Of course no silly woman would be capable of this vigorous moral exercise. But any one brave enough to subject herself to it, will find health returning and mental vigour increasing at a marvellously rapid rate. Great progress in colour-skill may also be attained by it; but a few simple rules must be adhered to.

Colour freely by the mere sensuous impulse of the eye, thinking meanwhile of something quite different, and paying no heed to any previously learned theories of Art.

Get the form, as much as possible, by the motion of

the hand, not looking at the needle-point. Use the eye only to select colour, and then to keep the work within certain bounds. The practice of following with the needle lines traced on the material with a pen or chalk is fatal to colour *inspiration* (not necessarily to colour *knowledge*); as the retina, fatigued by unnatural exercise, loses its sensitiveness to immediate colour-impulses.

If any tracing be used, let the design be as simple as possible, and purely Geometric. Trace on the back of the material, and run a thread through to the front. This thread will not need to be absolutely covered, as it can be afterwards removed.

If gold thread be used, wind it first on a reel, till it takes a curved set; shake it off the reel, and use the natural coils into which it falls, arranging these to please the fancy. Avoid using gold *over a tracing*. Some of the very ancient curves of Indian Art occur naturally when Japanese gold is *shaken* off a reel.

If the hand is stiff, it may be loosened and trained into tune with Nature's formative processes by the practice of drawing the Pentagram and Heptagram. I have the sanction of Dr. Maudsley for the opinion (which is confirmed by my experience) that this exercise is eminently suited to produce, in the muscles of the hand, a kind of automatic skill, a consonance with Nature's growth-processes, such as might well seem to primeval peoples miraculous. The copying of actual forms puts the hand into harmony with certain accidental outcomes of Nature's Laws; the Pentagram is an Algebraization of Nature's processes of development.

A good test whether the hand is properly in tune with Nature, consists in feather-stitching an irregular spray, in coarse silk, with the eyes shut. The spray so produced should be as natural-looking as anything that could be done with the eyes open.

I speak here of Needlework, that being the Art with which I am familiar; but similar principles to those above explained have been applied to colour-study with the brush. The fact that it is possible, by utilizing the polarity of nervous disease, to produce the peculiar old-Eastern colouring, and at the same time to facilitate cure by unifying the antithetic phases, throws light, I think, on the attitude of the Peutateuch writers, both towards colour-and-form Art, and towards the question of At-one-ment of error by return to the Unseen Unity. The Third Commandment might, I think, be for some persons paraphrased thus :—

When angry, do not indulge in blasphemous exclamations, or in wanton and exaggerated statements; but learn to curse and swear in colours. This will relieve your feelings as much as bad language could do, and will neither offend your neighbours nor injure yourself. It can be made a means of curing whatever evil tendencies may be latent in your nature, by employing them in the development of Artistic faculty. And be sure that God will bless every attempt to put yourself into line with His Creative energy; and will, sooner or later, punish every expression of evil which has no tendency to further its redemption to the service of Good and Unity.

There are those who smile at any serious treatment of so trivial a pursuit as Embroidery. But how can a woman be sure that she has truly grasped philosophic principles, unless she can employ them to improve feminine and domestic occupations? A wise man once asked : "How many angels stand on the point of a needle?" It is not recorded of any wise man that he was conceited enough to fancy that question could be lightly answered. The Father of the Calculus cautioned his readers not to despise The Infinitesimal; and a greater teacher even than Newton assured us that The Almighty does not disdain to reckon such trifles as the hairs on our heads. The Lord's People, of old, were encouraged to revel in mingling Gold and Blue and Purple and Scarlet; because it was felt that the combination of all incongruous colours into one harmonious Rainbow is a token (all the surer for being intangible and evanescent) that the Forces of destruction which threaten to overwhelm man shall be restrained for the salvation of those who trust in the Unity of God. For the Hebrew, the Rainbow was to be a token that God would interpose at last on behalf of His People. But our Father Odin taught that the Rainbow is a bridge, by trusting to which a brave soul can, on its own feet, so to speak, reach the home of the Divine.

CHAPTER XIV

THE SCIENCE OF PROPHECY

" Truth for ever on the scaffold,
　　Wrong for ever on the throne.
　But that scaffold sways the nations ;
　　And behind the dim Unknown
　Sitteth God within the shadow,
　　Keeping watch over his own."

A GREAT deal has been said and sung about the beauty of Truth, and its perpetual conflict with error. To the popular imagination Truth and Goodness represent themselves as a couple of knights-errant incessantly in the act of slaying certain dragons called errors and vices. It is supposed that whenever any one of these is, anyhow, destroyed, that is always so much gained towards the final triumph of Truth and Goodness over the whole noxious brood. But, alas! Truth and Morality, so far as man has to do with them, are conditions of brain, of a most exquisitely delicate organization. And just as it is possible to cure a comparatively harmless physical ailment by the use of remedies which lower vitality and tend to set up a more painful and more obstinate disease than they cure, so it is often possible to combat (and successfully combat) a bad condition of the mind by the use of means which leave it an easy prey to some worse condition. Those who would practice the art of curing physical disease are not allowed to content themselves with studying only the immediate action of remedies, so as to know what drug will neutralize what symptom; they are required to make themselves acquainted also with the structure of the human frame, and the nature of its reactions after certain modes of action, and even of hereditary reactions after stimulation. Those who take upon themselves to cure symptoms without knowledge of reactions are empirics or quacks. They are often wonderfully successful; but the result of trusting to them is a general depression of vital and recuperative power. He only is a true physician who so combats disease as to store up vitality; and he only is a true teacher who so combats evil as to store up brain-vitality. Therefore the Far-Seer, *i. e.* the student of the longer and slower mental reactions, often seems

to be opposing something which others think good.
The practical result of his peculiar study is that he can
rarely throw himself thoroughly into any violent " movement" for the salvation, education, enlightenment, or
amusement of mankind.	Prophets labour for Humanity
in their own way; but their way is seldom one that
contemporaries understand.	If we wish to realize why
such men as H. Spencer, Renan, Maudsley, Hinton, are
not noted for what is called Philanthropic Zeal, we must
ask ourselves why men of that stamp would not have
joined in the popular movements of the past.	There
was a time when wine was a new discovery.	It allayed
certain forms of suffering ; it ministered to the heightening of certain faculties ; clearly, then, wine was the gift
of a God ; men should drink it in reverent homage to
the Divine Giver, and show their gratitude by doing all
in their power to induce others to accept the gift.	Alas!
the Herbert Spencer of that day was only too sure that
there must come a reaction ; he could not become a
Bacchus-worshipper.	By and by the bad side of the
alcoholism revealed itself; Bacchus-worship was dis-
covered to be vice fostered by pious emotion.	The new
philanthropists preached a crusade against wine ; for
what could be more clear than that wine was bad ?
The Renan of that day could not become an advocate
of total abstinence ; he told his hearers that Bacchus-
worship must have had its good side, or it could not
have enlisted so many followers.	So it is now.	The
Prophet knows that much which is called Education
means forcing the young brain to give off, in wasteful
and useless display, the latent force stored up by our
ancestors ; that much which is called progress in civili-

zation consists in abandoning those processes of recuperation by which scientific men of old taught the masses
to store up latent energy for future use. Thus he who
sees ahead is a sceptic always; always a wet blanket
on the enthusiasms of those who only see to-morrow
or next year.

This gives a tone of sadness to the utterances of
Prophets. But the sadness is accidental, and due to
the fact of the subject not having been understood.
For in reality Prophecy is the most joyous and least
pessimistic of all Sciences. The Logos visits the follies
of the fathers on the children to the third and fourth
generation; but preserves what is good, for thousands
of generations; and all who know Him learn to realise
that such is the Law of His working.

Even this perception adds to the loneliness of the
Prophet; for as he irritates others by not being able to
share in their sanguine expectations of immediate
success, so he seems to them hard-hearted because when
they are most gloomy he cannot despair. He sees in
any misfortune that may occur, only the temporary
penalty (long foreseen by him) of man's over-confidence.
Through all depression the Prophet knows that the
Logos punishes for a small moment, but His mercies
endure for ever.

Another cause that adds to the loneliness of the Far-
Seer is that, sooner or later, he is almost sure to discover
a law which the young people about him desire not to
believe, viz. the wastefulness of original work published
before the complete maturity of the author. The best
work is that which combines Genius with Experience;
therefore the way to do the best work is to live to be

old. Original work is healthful exercise for the young; but the work of preparing one's own work for a public wears out the immature brain. Juvenile Genius is impatient, and clothes its own impatience in a disguise of devotion to Truth; but it would be better if that devotion took the healthy and unexhausting form of studying how to complete and preserve the work of predecessors. The consequence of impatience to be original is that the work of genius is done without experience; and that those who have genius comparatively seldom live to gain experience. There are, however, always a few who, though aware of their own original power, are willing to bide their time; and, few though they may be, natural selection always puts the balance of influence into their hands at last. But the feverish and impatient who rush forward to early success despise them for wasting time. And, unfortunately, many of the so-called reforms of modern education are taking the direction of encouraging young persons to expend their mental energy on original investigation, and discouraging reverent attention to the imperfect work of predecessors and teachers, the completing of which would be excellent preparation for more entirely original investigations. " Honour thy predecessors, *that thy days may be long in the land*," is the true secret of intellectual vigour. It would seem that, in the Eastern Schools of Prophecy, the younger Prophets were employed as messengers and interpreters between their elders and the outside world. This is excellent preparation for becoming, later on, Interpreters of the Unknown Truth to Mankind. The true pulsation of the intellectual life of an individual would appear to be, to utilize the age of passion for the purpose of gaining experience by helping older teachers; then, in fully ripe age, to fertilize the new generation with the best essence of one's own thought. And when a Prophet denounces a "curse" on young men whom impatient ambition makes neglectful of their elders, he is only speaking from the same scientific stand-point as a doctor who predicts future debility as the consequence of any physical sort of premature indulgence.

Several portions of this work were suggested by the conversations of Dr. Alfred Wiltshire, who had spent many years in the study of periodicity and of occasional reversal of attitude, as agents in the development of the human faculties, physical and mental. The foregoing paragraph is the substance of much which he said to me before his disease was apparent to others, but after he knew himself to be a doomed man. He told me that he had made his discovery of the danger of original work done young, too late to save himself; he hoped that his sorrowful experience might be of use in warning others.

The nature of my work precludes the possibility of specifying in detail the precise extent of my obligations to my various teachers. But one motive which spurs me on to complete it is the desire to keep the promise I made when Dr. Wiltshire was dying; that his children should know all I could tell them of the value of their father's life-work.

The most beautiful and powerful of all logical formulæ is also the simplest. It is the great Master Key of Prophecy; used, as such, by the mathematician Boulanger; and handed down, (for those who have eyes to

see) from our pious forefathers in the position of the
Mistletoe-berry.   No one who has ever used, or understood, this solemn formula would willingly translate it
into common words.   But so much misapprehension is
caused by the reticence which has been observed about
this and other formulæ of Grammarye that I, unwill-
ingly, state it here :—

We find the Germ of the Future when we look back
to where, in the Past, a branch separated and began to
grow into twin-twigs.

The difference between the Far-Seer and ordinary
educated men may be summed up thus :—Ordinary man
thinks of some condition or other as in itself good, and
desires to make that condition permanent.   If he be so
far educated that he consents to severe temperance in
such pleasures as those of food, it is because experience
has taught us that to make the enjoyment of such
pleasures short, periodic, and not too frequent, is the
best way to keep the system capable of enjoying what
are called " the higher pleasures," such as those afforded
by learning, religion, and the social emotions.   The
ordinary man thinks of physical temperance as a process
of sacrificing the lower pleasures to the higher ; he does
not understand that the rhythm of temperance should
be kept especially in what he calls the highest.   The
true Prophet, on the contrary, knows that *nothing* is
good except rhythmic alternation.   He is no more
a glutton intellectually than physically ; he no more
desires the constant enjoyment of what is called real-
izing the Presence of God than he craves for unlimited
brandy ; he no more aspires to a Heaven of constant
rapture in the intercourse of Jesus and the Saints, than

to a Valhalla of everlasting mead-drinking in the company of ever-lovely Valkyries. He desires, for every fibre of his body, and every convolution of his brain, and for all the faculties which he may hereafter acquire, that each may be the medium of an occasional revelation. And for every revelation he is willing to abide the time fixed beforehand by the Divine Revealer, from Whose Hands we never escape, even if we make our bed in Hell; and to know Whom is the only Heaven that we need, here or hereafter. And what he knows to be best for himself, that he believes to be best for his friends. He no more desires for his children incessant health or prosperity than he desires for his vines a uniform temperature. Therefore he seems to most people an unfeeling monster. Yet he is not unfeeling. His wife may perhaps desert him,[1] preferring the society of some man who is less advanced in the Science of Prophecy, and therefore more amusing and more outwardly cheerful (perhaps even, as seen from her point of view, more human and lovable). When this happens his heart breaks. But even when a heart is broken, his own or any one else's, the Prophet never forgets to take an awful joy in the fact that such experience is a Revelation.

Most men confess that they can know "God" only by faith; that all experience and actual personal knowledge would lead them no further than to know the "Devil," the Destroyer, the Avenger, the Tempter, the Accuser. The Prophet, too, knows this Destroyer; he differs from other men in this—that instead of inventing by faith a God *who does not destroy*, he knows the

---

[1] Hosea.

Eternal Destroyer as Eternal Love. Siva the destroyer, he protests, is co-equal and co-eternal with Brahma the Creator and Vishnu the Preserver ; and yet they are not three Eternals but One Eternal; not conflicting mysteries but one Ineffable palpitation ; not rival powers but One Loving Lord.

There is always about the true Prophet more or less of the feeling expressed by the daughter of the Asa-race in Tegner's immortal poem : " The King's daughter will not condescend to snatch at joy ; for she can fling away her whole life's happiness, even as a Queen can cast away her mantle, and still remain just what she was,—a Queen." The masses are jealous of a man to whom personal happiness is but a non-essential, and whose very indifference to his own fate confers on him the power of ruling those hampered with personal desires, by simply waiting till they have exhausted themselves in fruitless struggles after the fleeting joys of earth or the unattainable bliss of an imaginary Millennium. Their instinct tells them that his very existence is a danger to their prosperity. They crucify or burn him ; or they lock him up, at one time in a gaol, at another time in a mad-house, under the pretence that he " lacks the normal instincts," and on the assumption that they can know which instincts are " normal " and which are not so.

The Prophet's great danger is the tendency to fall into a mystic acceptance of evil. His faith and patience become exhausted in the struggle against other men's impatience to realize good ; he forgets that the true Good is not suffering, nor even the knowledge which suffering brings ; but the revelation of orderly Pulsation ; and that suffering where there should be joy is as much disorder as enjoyment where abstinence should be.

But underlying all that can be said about the difficulties of Seers in their intercourse with those around them, there is a latent fact of which the best physical expression is perhaps the irritable spring in the plant called *Impatiens Noli. me tangere.* By means of this spring, the seed is scattered, to germinate at a distance from the parent plant. The Prophet's knowledge is the outcome of all the most spiritual thought of his own country and age ; he can have no resting-place among his own people, because God means him to take a message to distant countries and to future generations.

Those who devote themselves to a study of the Pulsation doctrine naturally aspire to apply their knowledge to investigate the Laws of the throbbing backwards and forwards of that mighty engine, a mass of men animated by a common emotion.

CHAPTER XV

WHY THE PROPHET SHOULD BE LONELY

"It is good that one man should die for the People."

WE have been hitherto tracing the evils caused by the inability or unwillingness of the masses to enter into the thoughts of the Seers. We must now look at the other side, and try to see how dangerous to society is overwillingness to listen to the utterances of inspired Seers. Loneliness tends to save the Seer from becoming a charlatan, and to make of him a true Reformer. It

G

is, in fact, one of the most essential aids to true Reform and true Progress; for this reason :—Suppose that a reform is urgently needed in some particular. It is usually impossible to say beforehand in what exact mode it can best be made. Some man of genius tries experiments in his own little corner of the church or of society. If he is left alone to observe in peace the results of his attempts, then, after many years, he and those who have watched his career can say with authority which of his experiments were in the right direction, and which have been proved useless and need not be tried again. But if persons in official positions show favour to him at the beginning, it becomes the *fashion* to imitate him. Numbers do so who have no reason for it except that it is the fashion. The whole thing is made a party-question; and the thinker and those who are working under him become confused by counter-currents of senseless clamour. No chemist could, under similar conditions, conduct experiments in such simple matters as the purification of water or the improvement of cast-iron; far less can reforms in religion, in society, in thought, be organized thus. Moses, the great Reformer, after he had conceived his reform, is said to have retired into almost loneliness for forty years, and got no following till he had had time to mature his plans. And, in order that the people of Israël might be the true leaders in all Reform, he made rules which secure to each new Reformer something of the same isolation and silence; so that his crude attempts and immature conceptions may never be taken up as a mere fashion. Some people think these rules harsh; but they serve very good ends. They secure that showy, ambitious, self-seeking men[1] (if Jews) shall court advancement, either by deserting their church to get on in the Gentile world, or by an affectation of over-strict orthodoxy, by which they hope to win the favour of their own people. Either proceeding is contemptible in itself, but does the church little harm compared to what is done in other churches by showy, vain men playing at Reform. A Jew does not try experiments in Reform unless he is really devoted. The stern Jewish discipline secures for those who are trying social experiments something of the same isolation and quietness as those who are trying experiments in physical science secure for themselves by locking the laboratory door till they have found out what they want to know.

The scientific experiment lasts a few hours; the moral experiment the best part of a lifetime; and it seems hard to be ignored and unnoticed till old age. But no man should expect to sacrifice to the Lord that which costs him nothing. God accepts no sacrifice except that of our *best*. Whoever aspires to the honour of righting what has got wrong in the ways of a whole people must be content to be that of which the scape-goat was a sign; he must "bear upon him all their iniquities into a land not inhabited," and think and search in solitude as Moses himself did. The true Reformer must always be a man despised and rejected, in whom men see no wisdom; he must be shipwrecked, like Prospero, on a desert island, till he has perfected his methods. Then he can return, to rule the kingdom which is lawfully his own, the thought-realm of the

[1] This was written 20 years ago.

ideal; and the experiments of his ignorant days will not have disturbed the practical work of the Church among the masses who have no means of recreating the past from books in the domain of ideas; and for whom therefore the destruction of consecrated habits means too often spiritual death.

The sentence which condemns Reformers to comparative isolation acts like Gideon's test, in securing that the work of Reform shall be left in the right hands. He who has *seen* the Law of reaction vibrating down the ages, lives henceforth under a spell; for him, fate has no terrors, solitude no loneliness, and curses no meaning; he can go on his way notwithstanding any antagonism; he knows that, whatever may happen during his life, he will rule posterity from his grave. Those who *can* be stopped had better be stopped; they have not *seen* God.   One who knows so little about the ways of the Creator that he cares what contemporaries think, had better work on lines laid down beforehand; he should not go wandering off into the Infinite to seek new Truth.

Tegner[1] (whose conception of the value of ecclesiastical outlawry I am here following) represents the young champion of Reform and of Liberty outlawed, not because of any of the things which he wished or intended to do, but for *accidentally* setting fire to an old temple.   He is then subjected to a variety of tests, and gives such proofs of fidelity under difficult circumstances that at last he is elected king of a country adjoining the one from which he was banished.   But the spirit of his father reveals to him in a dream that he must not

---

[1] Frithiof's Saga.

venture to exercise even the function for which he has been chosen till he has made Atonement for his involuntary crime by rebuilding the Temple to which, in his rash young days, he set fire; and the Heathen priest who has heard of the lore of Judæa further instructs him that, if such reparation is to be accepted as true Atonement, the Temple must be dedicated, not to any partial Deity, but to the Unity who speaks through many messengers.

CHAPTER XVI

REFORM, FALSE AND TRUE

"The God *of your fathers* will bring you out of bondage."

THE difference between True Reform and mere fashionable quackery can be illustrated by example. In the beginning of the 19th century comparatively few English people learned foreign languages. At last some sensible people thought that it would be well if we in England knew more of the modes of thinking of our French and German neighbours. They made their children learn French and German, really for a reason—in order that the children should be able to converse with foreigners, and to read good books written abroad. That was a real Reform. Next it began to be the *fashion* to learn French and German. People who had neither the means nor the wish to procure foreign books took to neglecting all sound English education. Many country parents were satisfied with any sort of school in which a girl learned to repeat a few foreign phrases; they considered that proved she was educated in a superior and advanced manner. If such silly parents had been asked why a girl was to be made to pick up a smattering of French in preference to learning to understand English properly, they could not have told; "the gentry make their gals learn French;" they had no better reason. That is false Reform. There are Jews who are dropping that grand old inheritance, the Hebrew language, in order to get their children taught whatever happens to be in fashion. The Reform they are preparing is that their children will be formed on a lower type than that of their grand-fathers; about that, I think, there can be no sort of question. Re-form should always aim at *rise in type.* And this gives us the clue by which we can distinguish false Reform from true. A monkey will do anything, for no better reason than that some one else has done it *just before;* it is the privilege of men to study the memorials of the past, and to preserve them for future generations.

When I was a young girl I knew a farmer, who had in his house one of those old oak chests so much prized by lovers of Art, covered with beautiful carvings of scroll-work and flowers. The carving of one of those chests must have taken some man months, perhaps years, to do; and no one could have done it at all who did not really love his Art. Once done, such a piece of work is a delight to successive generations, and is prized as a family treasure. The farmer's mother became bed-ridden, and was obliged to hire a housekeeper to manage her house. This woman attended diligently to the dairy and all the practical farm-duties which she understood; but, not being interested in old carvings, she allowed the chest to become clogged with dust, so that the pattern could hardly be seen.   One day we called at the farm; the oak chest was missing.   In its place there stood a brand-new white box.   We asked for the oak chest. "What oak chest?" said the housekeeper.   "The one that used to stand in that corner."   "Oh! *that* old thing!   Why, he wur that old and shabby and dirty, as I were ashamed to see un; and the worms had got into un; so when the painters were doing up the front o' the house, I just fetched in a pail o' paint and a brush, and I tuk and I gived un a nice coat o' paint; and *don't* he look a beauty now?"   That good woman thought she had made a reform in the house, improved her mistress's property.   We all know that she was much mistaken. Her idea of improvement was a false one.

We have not all got old carvings in our possession; but we all have charge of some valuable old things; an old language, old customs, old traditions, old modes of thought which contain the stored-up mental force of our forefathers, old memories, a race-history, and some form or other of old religious faith.   And with all these things we can deal rightly, or we can deal with them wrongly. Changes of some sort we must have.   We must not keep every kind of old lumber in our houses, or there would not be room for ourselves.   We have to live our own lives; and we must not so crowd up the world with memorials of the past as to leave no room for the present.   We must sometimes make changes or there could be no progress.   Which changes are real Reform, and which are mere foolish fashion?   Then, again, just as an old carving left to itself gathers dust and damp and tends to decay, so everything that is old, if left to

itself, tends to become obscure and to moulder. Everything needs care to keep it fresh.   Much of our progress
consists in refreshing or renewing things that have grown
dusty with age ; the question is, How can this best be
done? We have then to study the two questions: What
is worth preserving? and :—How to preserve it ?   And
I think that if we give a few moments' attention to considering how the well-meaning servant above referred to
came to make such a mistake as she did, and what
exactly was the nature of her mistake, it may help us to
find our way to some of the great principles by which
false Reform ought to be distinguished from true.

First, how came she to make the mistake?   Well,
probably in some such way as this :—Either she herself
or some neighbour, when she was young, lived in
a room the walls of which were becoming dirty and
brown and scratched.   By and by it occurred to somebody to whitewash the walls.   And everybody who
came in said : " How you have improved the place !"
And the woman, then perhaps quite a child, got out of
the whole affair just this idea : When something is old,
and brown, and dirty, and has little holes in it, the way
to improve it is to put on it whitewash.   When she was
grown up and had charge of her mistress's furniture, she
neglected the oak chest because she took no interest in
it ; but all of a sudden it occurred to her that, if any
visitors called, it would look discreditable to have the
chest so dirty ; she did not care about the carving, but
she did not want to be disgraced in the neighbours' eyes.
The chest was old, and it was brown, and it had holes
and marks in which the dust lodged ; and it was dirty.
The old idea cropped up in her mind, from mere asso-

ciation, without reflection—"whitewash it, that's the way to improve it." She looked out of the window; there stood a pail of paint just handy, so she took it and did the deed; and in half an hour she had hidden from the sight of his posterity the loving, painstaking labour of a man who was dead and could not rise to interfere. Because somebody else improved a dirty wall with white-wash, she thought she could improve a dirty carving in the same way; because somebody else hid accidental scratches with whitewash, she hid, with paint, marks made by the loving care of a skilled carver.

Now if the woman's own father had carved the chest, if she remembered seeing him, when she was a child, working at it evening after evening, then, after he was dead, when it grew dirty and the dust began to clog the pattern, she would have carefully and lovingly brushed out the dust so as to make the pattern show. But she had not actually seen any one at work on it; therefore it never occurred to her to remember that somebody must have thought it worth while to spend time over the doing of it. It never occurred to her that she was blotting out the memory of the carver by destroying his work.

Here, then, is one clear principle by which to judge when to destroy memorials of the past, and how to refresh such as we decide to preserve. We should culti-vate "that power of imagination which forms so large a part of the Divine Charity," by learning to think some-times of our remote ancestors as if they were our imme-diate parents, and of the ancestors of others as if they were our own. We reverently consign to the fire many things possessed or made by our own parents, which had only a temporary value, rather than leave them littering about for no purpose except to cause annoyance and excite contempt; but we preserve and restore that which, by the exercise of a little care, can be made to have a permanent value and do our parents credit. In the same spirit we should deal with all the work of the past. Our old languages, old customs, old modes of religious observance, are often all that remain to tell us about serious, studious, devout men of long ago. It is easy to forsake old customs for the sake of following new fashions; but the consequence is, that hardly anything then will remain to tell our grandchildren what sort of people their ancestors were. And again, we should try to remember that comparatively little harm is done by the mere mistakes of individuals; all the most grievous mischief is caused by that massing of error which we call "fashion"; the unreasoning copying of what somebody else does without reflecting whether it is a suitable thing for us to do. Doing something new because somebody else did it, is not progress. Imitation without reason is the property of monkeys, not of men. Nothing is more dangerous to social order than the habit of imitating at random unselected examples. A thing may be very real progress when some one person does it for a reason; and the very same thing may be anything but progress if somebody else does it without a reason. We teach little children by imitation, but that is because they *are* children, because their reasoning powers are dormant. So we let a baby crawl on all fours till it can walk. But then a child has parents, who select what example they choose to put before its eyes, and who protect it from crawling into the worst kinds of mud.   The privilege of a grown man is to stand up on his feet and not crawl, and to think for himself what he ought to do, and whom he ought to imitate; and not copy the example of strangers without knowing why.[1]

CHAPTER XVII

CRITIQUE AND CRITICASTERS

"How beautiful are the feet of them that make Peace."

WE have traced some of the harm that is done by prejudiced rejection of new truth; we have also glanced at the far greater harm that may be done by over hasty acceptance of it. We have now to consider the question:—What are the steps which might be taken with a view to prepare the masses to receive in an orderly manner whatever new truths about the Pulsation of Life may in future be revealed; so as to secure the greatest amount of good with the least harm?   I do not propose to speak of any wholesale measures which need governmental action before they can take effect; but only to suggest possible endeavours for individuals. The present Chapter will relate to the Art of Critique, and address itself chiefly to those who have some experience of the work of teaching elementary mathematics. Any teacher of elementary mathematics might make his class work a real training in the Art of true Critique; and thereby not diminish but increase his success in his own proper subject.

[1]Given as a lecture at the Jewish Working-Men's Club.

Let us think for a few moments of the whole reading public as a College, which Truth, as Head-Master, is endeavouring to instruct and educate; and of men of Genius, discoverers, reformers, as assistant-masters, to each of whom is committed the task of teaching the subject of which he knows most. The comparison would be an impertinent one, if we illustrated it by reference to classes in such subjects as History or Language; because the school-teacher in such subjects is obliged to require from his pupils a kind of docility which readers are not expected to give to an author. But every mathematical teacher who deserves the name endeavours to accustom his pupils to take nothing for granted till it has been proved to their own personal satisfaction. The mathematician, therefore, is related to his class in much the same way as a writer to his readers. In my imaginary College, the various teachers are in the habit of attending each other's classes whenever they wish to do so; a practice which actually does prevail to a certain extent in some schools, and with the happiest results; for the teacher who takes his place among the pupils of a colleague, can, if he will, set the class an excellent example of courteous and intelligent questioning. But if the various teachers thought of each other's work in the same spirit as the leaders of Literature and Science do, and if the pupils thought of their teachers as the reading public do of writers and preachers, the result would be not only moral confusion, but intellectual chaos.

The chief reason why courtesy, reverence, and a *certain kind* of docility are needful for those who would learn, is this :—Truth is never received into the human mind without an admixture of conventions, of what may be called fictions. These fictions have to be introduced, used, and then withdrawn. It would be impossible to teach even so straightforward a subject as mathematics without the temporary use of statements which are not true to the nature of things. The history of a child who is learning mathematics, like that of human thought, is very much a record of alternate introduction of convenient fictions and subsequent analysis of their true Nature. A class, like a public, tends at times to become groovy and mechanical; to mistake the accidental for the essential; to treat necessary aids to learning as if they were actual truths; to lose sight of the relative importance of various kinds of information. A class in Botany tends to forget that classification and terminology are not so much part of the life of plants as circulation and fertilization; a class in Analytical Geometry forgets that the co-ordinates are no part of a curve. Just so, the reading public forgot, till Charles Darwin woke it up, that intermittence is no necessary part of Creative Action; although it is convenient for man, for purposes of classification, to *imagine* a series of intermittent acts. A student tends to such forgetfulness in proportion as he becomes mechanical in his work; the genius of a teacher is very much shown by the manner in which he contrives to arouse the interest and correct the errors of a class which is becoming too mechanical.

Theorists in education sometimes imagine that a good teacher should not allow the work of his class to become mechanical at all. A year or two of practical work in a school (especially with Examinations looming ahead) cures one of all such delusions. Education involves, not only teaching, but also training. Training implies that work shall become mechanical; *teaching* involves preventing mechanicalness from reaching a degree fatal to progress. We must therefore allow much of the actual work to be done in a mechanical manner, without direct consciousness of its meaning; an intelligent teacher will occasionally rouse his pupils to full consciousness of what they are doing; and if he can do so without producing confusion, he may be complimented and his class congratulated.

Let us now go into the subject more in detail. We teach laws of curves by reference to certain straight lines—tangents, co-ordinates, radii, etc. These lines bear the same kind of relation to the curves which the framework of sticks fastened into a pot bears to the climbing plant, which is the true object of the gardener's care. The plant itself is living and growing; the justification for the existence of the framework consists in the fact that it would be impossible to get the true enjoyment of the plant without its aid. The co-ordinates form no part of what we want to teach about; but we cannot learn without their help. They enable us to see how the curve came into being, and whither it is tending.

Suppose then that a class, while becoming skilful in working problems, seems to have forgotten that the axes are no part of the curve itself. The teacher may wake it up by saying, " You don't imagine, surely, that axes form any necessary portion of a curve. An ellipse, for instance, is the path of a body moving round a focus of attraction. Suppose a planet were endowed with the power of leaving a track in the sky, the track would be an ellipse only, unencumbered with axes. What are the axes, then? Indications of invisible forces? Not so. No line of attraction at any point of the orbit corresponds to the minor axis. The axes are *human devices* to enable us to measure and express the various elements of the orbit." "Well, but," exclaims perhaps some clever pupil, "if the straight lines are unreal, if they mean nothing, why were they invented, and why were we made to study them?" Such reasonable criticism is a great help to the teacher. He proceeds to picture the state of Astronomy in the days when nothing was known of the movement of the planets. He describes the first bewildered effort of the human mind to represent to itself the path of these wanderers. He shows how some man may have at last conceived the brilliant idea of projecting imaginary straight lines across the sky from one fixed constellation to another, thus forming a sort of background of measuring-rods; how the constellations, with these imaginary connecting lines, might be copied on a tablet, and the path of the planet registered thereon from day to day; and how Science might grow up by man inventing modes of measuring and registering curves which the living forces of Nature were describing in Space.

After such a lesson, the class goes on with its work with renewed interest and quickened intelligence. But how would the case be if a group of other teachers were present, who should comment on the lesson in this wise? One says "All the good books present curves with axes; you think yourself cleverer than our best writers." A second says, " It is perfectly crazy to attempt to teach people to think of curves without axes." A third says, " I really do think there is something in your view ; but this much is clear : when you accepted a post in this College, you undertook to use a standard text-book, and to teach on ordinary lines. If you have theories different from those generally accepted, you were at least bound to give up your post before you began to express them ; *then* we could have respected you. To stop here and to suggest doubts to the pupils is dishonest and scandalous ; and your conduct makes me doubt the honesty of everything you say." A fourth says, " You are right, and all the books are wrong. It is a shame that children should be taught to believe fictions ; away with these stupid books that have misled the world so long." A fifth is indignant that the grand old sages who created Astronomy should be accused of inventing falsehoods to serve their own ends ; the sixth, on the contrary, is angry that the time of the class should be wasted on listening to, and trying to follow, the mental History of a set of savages who lived before Analytical Geometry had become a Science. And some clever young lecturer, who happens to have heard that our solar system, as a whole, is in motion, and who fancies that such knowledge is his own peculiar property, triumphantly asserts that the earth-path is *not* an ellipse, but an elliptical spiral ; and that any statement based on the premise that the ellipse represents a planet-path must be false throughout. Now what chance would any of us have of teaching anything to a class subject to such interruptions of the normal current of thought ? In a College where such disorder prevailed, would the pupils be in a frame of mind to receive instruction? Would the teachers themselves be likely to preserve the calmness necessary for the investigation of Truth? That the picture I have drawn is no exaggerated one, that those whose mission is to arouse the public to a perception of the relation between the essential and the accidental have to run the gauntlet of a style of criticism as senseless and frivolous as I have represented, no one can doubt. We are all aware of the absurdity of our present modes of receiving new truth; few, I fear, are sufficiently aware of its evil effects. Therefore it is well for us to reflect what effect it would have on the teaching of so simple a thing as Geometry, if teachers introduced into each other's classes the element which is so rife in our literature.

True Critique is one of the fine Arts; as sacred and beautiful as all true Art. There is no keener pleasure for a good teacher than genuine criticism from a pupil. If a question is asked which shows that the teacher has failed to make intelligible a fact perfectly clear to himself, even that is a source of great enjoyment. But when, as sometimes happens, a remark is made which proves that we have not gone deep enough into our own subject, which opens up new avenues of thought, and forces us to reconsider a demonstration, to re-investigate a solution; when, in fact, the relation between teacher and pupil is for a time inverted, it is then that that relation becomes fullest of pleasure and profit. (And so of course it is, in a still higher degree, between a writer and the critical reader.) But what chance would a pupil have of making intelligent criticisms, or of asking suggestive questions, if it were the fashion

H

of the class to indulge in a carnival of absurdity wherein senseless accusations were flung about at random?

Let us return to the subject of Analytical Geometry.

The tangent to an ellipse is an imaginary straight line, representing the path which would be followed by the body tracing the ellipse, if its connection with the attracting focus were suddenly to cease. In its essence, the tangent is a sublime effort of the scientific imagination; it pictures the result of a sudden cessation of the action of gravity. In practice the tangent is a convenient line for indicating the curvature at any given point. The educational sentimentalists who object to mechanicalness, ought, if consistent, never to use a tangent in working a problem, without stopping to realize the grandeur of the idea involved. As a matter of fact, such incessant strain on the imagination and on the perception of the sublime is unhealthy and deadening. It is far better to use tangents, mechanically, as mere measuring-rods. But a good teacher will take care that no pupil goes through a year's work at Analytical Geometry without having been, once or twice, aroused to perceive the wonderful poetic conceptions represented by the lines he is using.

In our supposed disorderly College, a sentimental poet might take upon himself to reprove the Geometry teacher for allowing so awful a conception as the sudden cessation of gravity to be degraded by being talked of as a mere convenience, without due realization of its horror; a scientist holding utilitarian views might retort, that the function of the instructor being to impart *truth*, no such thing as the cessation of gravity ought ever to be mentioned before a class; because, as a matter of fact, no instance of any such event is on record.

Let us now pass to the subject of Arithmetic. Instead of fictitious lines, we have here to deal with fictitious statements, *i.e.*, with statements which, if treated as truths, are false, but which, when clearly understood to be mere convenient fictions, do actually convey truth. Such a statement, for instance, is, " Twelve pence equal one shilling." No one is ever really deceived by this particular statement; but that is because all are familiar with the actual coinage, and know that, as a matter of objective fact, " a shilling " is not identical with " twelve pennies " (in the sense in which " a dozen apples " is identical with "twelve apples"). But a similar statement, made about unfamiliar objects, or about abstractions, might be misleading, unless the teacher took care to prevent misconceptions. And even in the case of our familiar coinage, it is essential to good mental discipline that the pupils should occasionally be made to define carefully the sense of the word " equal," in the sentence " twelve pence equal one shilling," and have their attention directed to the fact that, if accepted as true, it becomes false; that it contains and conveys truth only while clearly understood to be a fictitious but well-arranged convention. If the teacher forgets to do this, he ought to be grateful to any one who reminds him of his omission.

Now let us suppose that, in our imaginary College, the pupils are unacquainted with the actual coinage, and the teacher not sufficiently awake to the meta-physical necessity for defining, for them, words the real meaning of which is present to his own mind. He simply states: "Twelve pennies are one shilling." A lecturer on physics may afterwards happen to make a statement, the obvious outcome of which is that twelve pennies are (in weight) equal to about twenty-one shillings; and a chemist might prove that silver and copper are not identical, and that no amount of silver can produce the medicinal properties or chemical reactions of a grain of copper. Each teacher will then have made a statement, judged by which his two colleagues will each have spoken falsely. Such a thing is quite conceivable as that a party-spirit should arise in the College; the pupils each taking the side of his favourite professor, and accusing the others of gross ignorance or of wilful per-version of truth. The unlucky mathematician might *then* do what he ought to have done, but forgot to do, at first, *i.e.*, point out that he was using the word "equal" in a conventional sense; a sense perfectly legitimate for his purpose, though legitimate only within the scope of that purpose. But if party-spirit had already been aroused in the matter, and angry or contemptuous accusations flung about, the explanation would only add to the confusion; for the teacher would now be accused by the adverse party of paltering with truth, of using words in a double sense with intention to mislead; his very explanation would be quoted against him in triumph as a confession of guilt. Again I ask, what chance would the teachers in such a College have of discovering truth, or the pupils of learning what had been discovered?

A very prevalent form of criticasterism might be parodied as follows:—The teacher states a question thus: "The rate of exchange is 9½*d.* for a franc; how many francs shall I receive for so many shillings?" A colleague interrupts the lesson to ask what evidence there is to show that this is the exact rate. Another asserts that the last rate quoted was 9·875d. per franc; and a third insists that the last quotation was 9·876d. They engage in a vehement discussion of the point; but all agree that such gross ignorance of facts as the teacher betrays, proves him to be incompetent; and that, as the statement on which his procedure rests is proved false, his whole chain of reasoning falls to the ground.

I will close these mathematical illustrations by narrating an incident which actually occurred. An intelligent girl, who had been badly taught arithmetic, joined my class. I set her a sum about some damaged articles worth, originally, £3 15s. each, but which were to be sold in a lump at an abatement of one pound and some shillings on the price of each. She was required to find what would be received for the whole. It so happened that the lump sum amounted to so many pounds and *fifteen shillings*. She came to me saying that she could not get her sum right; the shillings were right, but the pounds were wrong. I worked it for her; beginning, of course, by subtracting the shillings of the abatement from the original fifteen shillings. " But I *had* the shillings right," she cried; "now you are getting it *all* wrong!" There was something very touching in her dismay at seeing the poor little bit of rightness, which she had secured, put wrong, and I felt like a ruthless destroyer of the last refuge of an innocent soul; but Arithmetic tolerates no sentimental hesitations; and I had, of course, to persist. At last, by trusting in blind faith to accurate Logic, we got the whole right, to her great surprise. I asked her to explain her own method.

It appeared that she had first set down the original price as given in the book, and then looked at the answer in the end of the book, and, finding that the shillings there corresponded with what stood before her on her paper, she copied them straight into the "Answer" place, thinking that it would be useless (and, I am sure, *feeling* vaguely that it would be irreverent) to meddle with what the book pronounced to be right. She had therefore set to work to manipulate the pounds with a view to get *them* into accordance with the official standard! Of course she failed. Of course,—from our point of view; but from hers, it seemed that *adhering to the book as long as you could* must be the right thing to do! I was then able to explain to her a little about the right use of authoritative standards; to show her that, if used as a check on results, they may often be of use by revealing errors in our reasoning which might other- wise have passed unperceived; but that, if taken advantage of to spare ourselves the effort of working out our own problems at our own cost, they are gener- ally found misleading. My pupil profited, I hope, by the lesson, in more ways than one. But what chance should I have had of teaching her either arithmetic, or the right use of standards, or anything else, if any other teacher had confused her mind, before I had half finished my explanation, by reproving me for teaching her to rebel against the authority of the text-book, and to work sums as she liked, without reference to the only infallible standard; and by warning her that I was only pandering to license and carelessness?

"Truth for ever on the scaffold; wrong for ever on the throne." The scaffold on which Truth is murdered, the throne on which wrong sits to rule, are built of careless, irreverent, senseless criticisms. When the account of the good and ill which we have done on earth is summed up, the heaviest item in the account against many of us will perhaps consist in the record of our *idle words*.

The aim of all students should be, so to pass through things temporal that finally they lose not the Eternal; so to pass through temporary aids to knowledge as not to miss perceiving the Eternal Truths. Only unpractical dreamers suppose that Truth can be grasped without adventitious and fictitious aids; all true students know that they are dependent on such aids; and their hope is so to use them as not to abuse them. We are in danger of becoming entangled in these adjuncts of Truth; of mistaking them for actual truths. Therefore The Unseen Wisdom which guides the destinies of mankind, raises up occasionally what we call "a *Reformer*"; whose function is to give to Humanity such a lesson as I have described the teacher of Analytical Geometry giving to a class. The Reformer reminds us that our framework of aids to investigation is not, in itself, Truth. As the mathematician teaches us to see the actual path of a planet, in contrast, on one hand, with the tangent conceived by imagining an impossible state of things from which the action of Gravity is suspended, and, on the other hand, with the Axes which are well-arranged measuring-rods, so the Reformer teaches us to look at the actual Life of Humanity, in contrast, on one side, with the Vision of an impossible Idea made simple by the omission of certain elements, and, on the other side, with that convenient mechanism by which the comprehension of our duty is facilitated for us.

How our Heaven-sent Reformers are received, we know : Truth on the scaffold ; and, on the throne, whoever helps us to confuse convenient fiction with fact. The world is surely old enough to behave less like a class of ill-bred school-boys than it has as yet done; it might prepare itself to give to its future Seers a reception more worthy than it has given to Seers in the past. All we who are engaged in mathematical teaching may contribute to that end, if we take pains to make our pupils distinguish between Truth and the mere accessories of study. We may also do something to train the rising generation in a comprehension of the difference between true and false criticism; we may accustom them to combine the fearless loyalty which compels a learner to express frankly his real difficulties and doubts with the respectful courtesy which checks irreverent and thoughtless cavil.

CHAPTER XVIII

THE SABBATH OF FREEDOM.

" Let not the son of the stranger that hath joined himself to the Lord, say, The Lord hath utterly separated me from His people ; for thus saith the Lord : The sons of the stranger, that join themselves to the Lord to serve Him, every one that keepeth the sabbath and taketh hold of My covenant ; even them will I bring to My holy mountain, and make them joyful in My house of prayer."

ISAIAH lvi., 3-7.

IF we visit a well-conducted Gymnasium in a school, we find rhythmic pulsation exhibited in the exercises in more than one form. In some, a limb is sharply thrown out from the body, and immediately and rapidly withdrawn. In others, the pupils assume slowly some extreme and even exaggerated position; usually one which would be condemned in the class-room as disorderly. Now it does not occur to the Lady Principal to reprove the teacher for thus reversing the orders given by her, nor to bring an accusation of defying her commands and teaching the pupils to set her authority at naught. On the contrary, all parties concerned know that the very object of School-Gymnastic is to undo the cramping effect of class-room discipline. For a young child, or a wild beast, which spends many hours daily in exercise, no gymnastic is so good as the free play of all its limbs; but as soon as the business of life imposes the necessity for a cramping specialization, mere play, during the short hours allowed for relaxation, is no longer sufficient to give freedom and elasticity to the frame; the exercise must be specially adapted to counteract whatever forms of specialization may be imposed during the hours devoted to work. Every one knows this, and nobody objects. Every teacher knows that unity among the staff, so far as physical education is concerned, implies, not agreement in opinion as to the best position for girls to place themselves in, but what may be called a "*consensus of reverence for the harmony produced by organized antithesis.*" *Life* means not this position or that, but *alternation* of position. No faculty or organ is properly fitted for its appointed work till it has trained itself, or been trained, into a possibility of rhythmic action; and education means chiefly the bringing one faculty after another into subjection to this cosmic law.

Long before this principle had been clearly seen to

apply to physical education, Philosophers knew that it was the principle of healthy mental action.   Laws of Thought are discovered far earlier in the world's history than Laws of things; for the reason given in Chapter XI., *viz.*, that every man who is capable of thinking can, if he will, state the Laws of Thought with absolute exactness and certainty; whereas Laws of things are only arrived at after centuries of observation of phenomena; and even then, as Mr. Boole explains, the statement is, to the last, a hypothetical and probable one (until we have succeeded in Algebraizing the Law of the becoming of the things).   It was known that the principle of *contradiction* (or free pulsation) is the life of the mind, many centuries before medical men had discovered that in it consists the life of the muscles.   Logic should be to the mind what gymnastic is to the body; a practice in reversal of attitude.   Yet, for some singular reason not yet explained, the mass of teachers and statesmen, while they encourage the application to the physical life of the principle of rhythmic alternation, either deny, or more frequently ignore, that it has any place in the moral life.

The reason appears to be this:—Parents, teachers, and governments wish that children should develop *the power to assume at will any physical position.*   Teachers and governments are content with such control of the physical as enables them to secure the public safety and order.   But few teachers or governors are content with safety and order in moral affairs; they wish to retain in their own hands a far greater control of mental and moral action than this.   The more healthily developed the frame is, the easier it is to preserve a statuesque repose *during certain specified hours;* but only a cramped and sickly organization can be kept *continuously* in one position. Healthy mental gymnastic makes children willing law-abiders and docile pupils during the hours of lessons; but it emancipates them, by making impossible continuous interference with their mental freedom. Now a privileged class can better maintain its power over a sickly and vicious population than over a population of orderly free-thinkers.

A detestable practice prevails in Christian England, and is, I regret to say, on the increase, of teaching in Sunday-school after the same method as is found on week-days to answer the purpose of preparing children to pass Examinations successfully. The material of the lessons is changed on Sundays, the attitude is not; for the History of Rome or France is substituted that of Palestine; for the Logic of Aristotle that of Paul; for the Poetry of Shakspere that of Isaiah; the change is apparent, the monotony is terribly real. The children are subject, throughout their teaching, to the same grinding pressure. Surely religious people of all sorts might join in trying to put a stop to this hideous prostitution of the Blessed Sabbath to the purposes of making children slavish and helpless; and claim it for the purpose for which it was originally instituted,—the cultivation of freedom by *reversal of attitude.*

As for the manner in which reversal of attitude may be induced, that must depend on the subject which is occupying attention during work-hours. If a boy be engaged in weeding, the teacher of his Sabbath-school should point out to him that crops and weeds belong equally to the vegetable kingdom, and have many characteristics in common; that the Parsnip even belongs to the same class as Hemlock, and the Turnip to the same class as the weed Shepherd's Purse; that the plants are equally good in the sight of God, and equally interesting from the point of view of Science; that the fact of some plants being fit for human food, and others useless or harmful to man, is due to an accident of the human organization. The weeder should be exhorted to *make a practice* of preparing for repose by reflecting a moment on these truths as he comes home from work in the evening. He should be told, too, that the amount of blessing which he can thus draw down on himself by meditating on The Unity of plant-life, will be commensurate with the completeness of his attention, during work-hours, to the business of discriminating crop from weeds.

This lesson forms a good preparation for the great climax of all unification. The pupil should be told that the business of our life on earth consists in weeding Good from that which, for man, is Evil; and that we should prepare for the Sabbath, by which the strain of life is relieved, by thinking of Him of Whom it is written: "I make Peace, and I create evil, saith the Lord."

For a kitchen-maid, a suitable unification would be to reflect on the fact that the potato and its peel,—or the cabbage and its outer leaves,—grew *as one.*

For a class in History, the unification might consist in reflecting that the Nation whose exploits they have been admiring, and whose triumphs they have been sharing, is but a part of Humanity; that every victory it has won, in war, has injured some other Nation; whereas every achievement it has made in Science or Art has, sooner or later, enriched the whole human race. This act of sympathy with Mankind as a whole will be more productive of vigour, in proportion as the pupils have, during the History lesson itself, thrown themselves more unreservedly into the emotions of the particular people of whom they are reading.

At Queen's College I tried for some years the experiment of holding, on Sunday evenings (the only available time; but the eve of Sabbath would have been more suitable), a true logic-class for the resident pupils. That I made many mistakes I need not say; the whole subject was, at that time, entirely in the condition of pure theory; and I had, as I went on, to find out what were the practical difficulties. Moreover, the College was under clerical management, and of all the staff, including the council and committee, only two members ever had the faintest idea what I was trying to find out, or why I went to the place at all. I had therefore to be very careful not to suggest doubts of the wisdom either of clerical authorities generally, or of our own in particular. The position was difficult, but I tried to find out whatever I could. On week-days the girls had, of course to attend to one subject at a time, and to look at each from a prescribed point of view. On Sundays I read to them any book, or allowed them to talk of any subject, that seemed to interest them, and encouraged the free play of their minds; but I took care to lead the conversation into the channel of finding what light one subject of study throws on another. The characteristics of the week-day lessons being *submission* and *specialization*, I made those of the Sunday lessons *free expansion* and *unification*.

Old pupils assure me that they never discovered any jarring contradiction between my views and those of our clerical heads. The substance of their comments is much as follows :—" I didn't know you were teaching us anything on those happy Sunday evenings ; I thought we were being amused, not taught. But after I left College I found you had given us a *power*. We can think for ourselves, and find out what we want to know." Now what was Sabbath instituted for, and what was Logic made for, except to create free-thinkers, free men and women, intellectual athletes, Prophets, and, in the best sense of the word, priests? Moses wished that all the Lord's People should be Priests and Prophets, even as he was.

It is almost needless to remark that the result indicated is due to the observance of a *Sabbath* of Freedom, sharply contrasted with week-day discipline. No such good effects follow the practice of leaving girls to think at random, and to study what they choose (or not study at all), all the week long.

I would never again try to teach under similar circumstances. The logician should not be a servant of a clerical body. If any true mode of teaching Logic became general, it would gradually modify all religious teaching, and make it tend to become a training in order and reverence, not an inculcation of opinions or prejudices. Few clergymen would preach such sermons as they now do, if they knew that their arguments were subjected each week to a careful logical analysis, and all the reasons for the contrary opinion to their own were pointed out before the younger members of their flock. In fact, the same change would pass over religious and moral teaching as has passed over the teaching of physical deportment. A mother or governess now has to be content with forbidding certain attitudes as unsuited to the drawing-room or class-room ; she cannot go through the solemn farce of forcing on the child her prejudices about certain attitudes being in the abstract "unladylike," when she knows that the child will presently be made to assume those attitudes by order of the Gymnast. So a clergyman would, if Logic were properly taught, be obliged to content himself with inducing in Church an attitude of reverence and devotion ; he could not, with a grave countenance, attempt to inculcate his own opinions or prejudices as essential truths.

The command that children should honour their own parents by no means implies that they are not, once a week at least, to be put into an attitude of sympathy with the ideas of other people. This teaching of true Logic in no way tends to interfere with the submission due, in matters of fact, to parents or other lawful authorities. On the contrary, it makes submission seem less harsh. Disobedience in a child is usually the result either of unsatisfied craving for that reversal of physical posture which is the life of the muscles, or of unsatisfied longing for that antithesis of mental position which constitutes the life of the brain. When we attribute naughtiness in a child to the natural depravity of his own heart, we often might more truly attribute it to the unnatural depravity of some adult, who has made him ill by trying to prevent his reversing either the physical or mental attitude in which she placed him.

Religious writers are expected to have something to say on the subject of Incarnation. The present writer mentions it here, only in order to show that she is not afraid of it.

Incarnation is, necessarily, *phenomenalization ;* for it is the manifestation of somewhat. The Incarnation believed in by Christians is necessarily one-sided ; for it is the manifestation of *Good*—of those qualities, in a perfect form, which, in an imperfect condition, constitute what we call human goodness, without any admixture of the fierceness and lust which God created in brutes, but which, in man, are evil. Neither the existence nor the value of such a crowning of all phenomenalization has been denied by our great mathematical Logicians. Babbage and De Morgan, Gratry and Boole, concurred in thinking the subject of Singular Solution worthy their profoundest study. But its value is as a type-model for us, an intellectual and moral guide for our working-hours. The notion of substituting, on Sabbath, prostrate adoration of a Manifestation of one side of God, for meditation on the Ineffable and Inconceivable Union of polar attributes, is one which Logic cannot take seriously into account, and which Logicians can find no words to characterize.

The earliest Christians kept Sabbath *as Jews*, and consecrated the working-week by a First-day communion with Jesus ; which shows that they took a logical and sane view of their relation to their Master. Whatever excuses priests may afterwards have made to the conscience for ignoring altogether the main purpose of Sabbath, the latent motive for it must have been the same which had prompted all similar perversions. As

Boulanger says,[1] no inefficient government can possibly maintain its place, unless the masses can be induced to adopt some form of idolatry; for the worship of The Inconceivable Unity confers such elastic strength, that a people accustomed to it would at once shake off any government which no longer represented its own highest Ideals. And every inefficient government instinctively has recourse, if it can, to the device of using as tools for the brutalizing of the masses, those very priests whose original function was to vitalize the masses. " Priests were appointed to lead man in the right road; but in all ages they have feared lest he should find it and walk in it. . . . Men have believed that they could, without degradation, behave as the slaves of Him Who set us free; and" (as the true God retires before such unworthy homage) " they have only succeeded in becoming slaves to His hypocritical Ministers." Thus does Boulanger sum up the History of Religion; and thus may be summed up all that Logic can have to say about any teaching of so-called *Religion* which aims at preparing pupils for Examinations, or which adopts methods found useful in preparing for examination in "secular" subjects.

CHAPTER XIX.

THE ART OF EDUCATION.

" The heathen say, Where is your God ?"

METHODS of teaching which, from the point of view of medical psychology, are sound (*i.e.*, those which vitalize and sanitate the brain), are distinguished from vicious

[1] *Origine du Despotisme Oriental.*

methods (*i.e.*, those which exhaust the vital powers and create bad habits of mental sequence) by the fact that the former are conformed to the central or fundamental law of Thought-sequence.

The physiology teacher lays on his table two specimens of the same bone; one from which all the gelatine has been boiled, and the other from which the phosphates have been discharged by acid, leaving only a gelatine shape. The class are instructed to examine each separately, and then to form a mental picture of a bone in which these two structures mutually interpenetrate each other. The teacher probably supposes himself to be merely illustrating the structure of bone; but in reality he is illustrating the fundamental law of sound mental action. Would that all teaching was done on the same model! We should then hear very little about " breaking down from over-work in schools!"

The bone-lesson above referred to gives the standard model on a very minute scale; education should copy that model on various scales of size. The rhythmic beats of alternate specialization and synthesis may vary from the five minutes or so occupied by the bone-lesson, to a period of a whole year; they should be of various degrees of complexity; from learning to see as one, two aspects of the same bit of bone, to learning to see what light the year's lessons on History, Language, Mathematics, and Physical Science throw on each other's meaning. The most important rhythm would appear to be one whose pulsation occupies about seven days.

Gratry has pointed out how the habit of periodic synthesis of different branches of study strengthens the mind and enables it to do a marvellous quantity of work without exhaustion or injury. He also calls attention to the fact that when this habit of periodic synthesis is once gained, the brain does a good deal of it by some process of unconscious cerebration, and even during sound and refreshing sleep.

The principle on which Gratry's system, and every other vitally healthy one, depends, is that mere cessation of action, or even mere change of action, is not rest; rest must be prepared for by *antithetic* action. The normal sequence of the lungs is expansion, contraction, repose. If we tried to make our lungs stand still at any point of the cycle except the right one, such inaction would not give true rest, but induce disease. So it is with all our functions; each organ must not only have its period of non-action, but it must be prepared for inaction by completing its cycle of action, or else the inaction is not sufficient rest. The true brain cycle is this :—

Forming special conceptions; unifying those conceptions; washing out all conceptions by thinking of The Inconceivable Unity, Repose.

Sabbath and Jubilee mean not *inaction*, but *renewal*. Sabbath was, in fact, in its origin, the Festival of The Unity; the true key-note was struck in the "Preparation for Sabbath"; recreative rest was to be prepared for by reaction against specialization, by seeking to know The Unity.

If ever parents understood the Art of mental recreation by Unity, the school-teachers must have had reason to feel that their lines had fallen in pleasant places! Teaching, especially for the more conscientious teachers, is made very unsatisfactory by the general lack of recognition of the true Art of recuperation ; for this reason:—

The exercise of any organ or faculty takes place by converting its latent force into active force, which is then given off in the form of "function" (*i.e.*, the action appropriate to the organ or faculty). That this exercise strengthens instead of weakening our faculties, is due to the fact that the withdrawal of latent force by exercise creates an immediate receptivity for new force, which then becomes latent. And, under all ordinary conditions, the new supply taken in is in excess of that given off. This new supply ought to come from extra-human sources (including, of course, but not exclusively consisting of, food and air). A sound method in Education means, chiefly, a method which secures that the recuperation shall come from these extra-human sources. But a teacher may be brilliantly successful at Examinations without understanding how to effect this, or caring to try. There are several non-legitimate ways by which he may be securing his apparent success. He may be draining either the physical vitality of his pupils, or those intellectual faculties which are not needed for the pursuit of his own subject, or the moral faculties, especially those for the exercise of which school-life affords no great scope, but which will be needed for the conduct of adult life. Now when a faculty is thus passively drained at second hand, it suffers the same loss of force as if it were itself exercised; and it is not stimulated to healthy recuperation. Therefore the "successful" teacher may, in reality, be either destroying the physical health of his pupils, or *preventing more conscientious and less showy colleagues from attaining the amount of success which they deserve*, or preparing his pupils to be bad men and women, and a source of moral corruption; or he may be sowing the seeds of what, in later life, will develop into what is even legally actual insanity. He may do any or all of these things without ever uttering a word in the hearing of pupils on any subject except the one he professes to teach.

From all that Gratry and Boole have said, it would appear that the question whether the faculties exercised recuperate themselves from extra-human sources, or by draining away the vitality of other faculties, especially the moral stamina, depends mainly on whether the synthetical work is commensurate in amount and kind with the specialization, and is properly alternated with it.

The process of synthesising the work of the week is by no means difficult, even for the teacher; and to the pupils it appears like mere amusement. There are two reasons why it is neglected. One is that any unification at all commensurate with the amount of specialization now going on in schools, is looked on at present (in England at least) with dread. Whenever those who understand the process try to call attention to its importance, the subject is almost sure to be treated, by those who do not understand it, as if we were talking of what is technically called " religion," and trenching on ground which is the proper domain of parents and the clergy. The thing which I mean (or rather which such Logicians as Gratry and Boole have, in all ages, meant) has no more connection with what is called " religious instruction," than it has with Algebra or Grammar. We mean the mental *act* of synthesis, which forms the compensating recoil from the specialization induced by study ; completing the pulsation, of which special studies form one-half; and causing whatever faculties have been used in special studies to draw their force from the extra-human sources, instead of draining the vitality of other faculties.   At present the Sabbath, so far as it is used at all, is appropriated to the teaching of the special study called "religion" (*i.e.*, *the history of the lives and opinions of 'former synthesizers*); and no adequate provision is made for mental *acts* of synthesis on the part of the pupils themselves.   Such synthesis as they are taught to do, is left to chance and to individual teachers.   Boole's Text-Book of Differential Equations is, in its way, a model of what can be done, within the compass of a particular subject, towards alternating special study with synthesis.   But, within that compass, there is no scope except for time-synthesis (*i.e.*, the study of the History of the subject), which in Boole's book alternates with the study of the subject itself.   The book has been superseded ; more modern ones serve more effectually the purpose of preparing for Examinations.   Gratry has received little attention from ordinary teachers.   His splendid analysis of the effects of synthesis alternating with specialization, in giving vitality, is mixed up with details of the special plan of sequence in study by which he secured the alternation for himself.   Now Gratry's sequence could not be accurately followed in any school ; it could not be attempted in any school which prepared pupils for Examination.   Therefore commonplace teachers ignore him altogether, and the course of Natural Selection throws all the benefit of Gratry's discoveries into the hands of teachers who have intellect enough to seize his main idea and disentangle it from his special plans.

So with regard to Boole's text-books.   The time-synthesis (or so-called historical method), of which he exhibits samples, is a very good thing in its way, failing anything better. But the specialist teacher, even if he knows this method, can only use it within the limits of his own subject; and it must be, at best, utterly inadequate to compensate the strain of modern education and restore the needed amount of energy. No one was better aware of this than the Author himself. Nothing is really adequate, except a periodic synthesis class, in which a synthesis of all the week's work is made *by the pupils themselves*, under the guidance of a competent Logician. And it is essential to full success that no subject which has been forced on the attention of the pupils *by any specialist teacher whatsoever* shall be forbidden ground at the Logos-class. I use the word " Logos " in preference to *Logic*, because the latter term has been taken to imply a special kind of study. Logos is the old word for the thing of which I am speaking, the Logic of the Logan-stone; the blessed antithesis to those fixed stones of evil magic and arrested progress which show the consequence of not keeping Sabbath.

The much vilipended Examination-system has the great advantage of preventing the possibility of carrying out the *plan* of any Idealist *as conceived by him*. It forces us, therefore, if we would learn anything from the ideal purists, to understand thoroughly those principles of sanitation from which their plans are projected; so as to be able to create our plans for ourselves according to circumstances. Strange as it may sound, I venture to prophesy that the Examiner will prove, in the long run, the best friend of Idealism in Education, by making a clean sweep of all second-hand imitators of Idealist thinkers.

The whole notion of leaving the selection of a Logos-teacher to the caprice or ignorance of individual parents, would be, of course, absurd. The essence of his function is the re-uniting of strains of thought which have been forcibly separated by the school-work. The first condition of his performing it is that he should know something of the methods employed in the School. Properly speaking, the Logos-Class should be held by the Head-Master or Mistress. If that is impossible the substitute should be thoroughly in the confidence of the Head.

A second reason why synthesis is insufficiently taught, is that it gives to the teacher an *appearance* of mere Nihilism; he seems to be Socratically neutralizing everything and actually teaching Nothing. This Nihilism is only apparent; the general and ultimate effect is in the highest degree both conservative and constructive. But that specialist and positive teachers always *feel* the work of the synthesizer to be antagonistic to theirs, there is no denying. Long ago it was said that "the heathen" (by which was then meant the antagonists of Logos-teaching) said to the Prophets of the Formless and Invisible Unity: "Where is your God?" (or, where is your Good?) Oken's answer to this question is almost brutal in its cynical audacity:—

$$God = Zero.$$

Boole puts his statement into a less startling form; but it comes practically to the same as Oken's: $x(1-x) = 0$; which means:—When you have selected your integral unity, or Universe of Thought (however large or small), and divided it into any two sections, x and *not-x*, if you then interpenetrate with each other the two conceptions, the result is zero. If any other result presents itself, your brain action has been imperfect.

The old Hindoo sages knew that we can form no idea of Deity except by affirming and then denying every quality in turn. A *thing* cannot, at one time, be black and white, except of course in different parts; yet to formulate aright a statement about God, we must say that He at once possesses every conceivable quality and its opposite, and yet has no parts. In other words

God is No-Thing.

Impatient ignorance asks, of course, " *Cui bono?* " "Who is better for the whole laborious proceeding of Meditation, if there remains NOTHING to show for it?" The answer is that neither Oken's Zero, nor Boole's, has any connection with negation or non-existence. That Zero means: "No form, but a living Force; No-Thing, but a power of understanding, utilizing, and even creating things." The result of a proper synthesis-lesson is, not the knowledge of any theologic proposition which can be stated in a neat sentence at a Divinity-Examination; but an increased power of understanding the genesis and structure of facts generally, and an improved hygienic condition of brain. The pupil, in fact, gets out of the unification-lesson a supply (commensurate with his week's work) of *Creative Energy.* Idealists such as Gratry and Boole are too prone to wonder what more any man can want, for this world or the next, than just *that*, and then plenty more of the same. Practical teachers, however, know very well that man in general wants *recognition by his fellow-man.* He wants, in fact, *success;* that visible success which can only be attained by the use of some method which is, metaphysically-speaking, imperfect. Beneficent Nature, who implanted this desire in the teacher-mind, is wiser than the Ideal purists; she has made abundant provision for its legitimate gratification. Any clever teacher has a right to use any method he likes, and to become as successful at Examinations as he can. It is the business of the child's "Pastor" (not the preacher of a special religion, but the Shepherd-servant of the Unity) to harmonize all the special aberrations by a suitable periodic synthesis. He will seem to neutralize the work of the teachers. He will especially seem to be neutralizing the work of any teacher who either introduces a new method, becomes rapidly popular, is very successful in preparing for Examinations, or, above all, possesses Genius of a showy order. Genius and originality are dangerous factors in education, unless their action is counteracted by a specially suitable synthesis. But the more dangerous a method of teaching is when not suitably counteracted, the more capable it is of becoming a source of vitality when it is suitably synthesized. The very alternation between a method which is highly vicious (*i.e.,* which rapidly produces showy results), and one which is sound (*i.e.,* produces no results except accession of force), this alternation, when habitual, sets up its own glorious pulsation, and generates by induction a force, perhaps the very highest and most vital which Humanity can command. The danger of modern education does not consist in the imperfectness of imperfect methods; it is that no provision is made in the mental life for alternating their use with that of

those perfect methods the result of which is " Nothing "
—except force stored up for the specialist teachers to use.
In the physical life it is now perfectly understood that
it is some teachers' business to produce no result except
a neutralization of the harm which is incidentally done
by other teachers as a necessary concomitant to the good
they are doing. Fifty years ago any one who had
ordered young ladies to put their hands on their hips,
then on their toes, and to assume, in fact, every position
condemned by their parents and teachers as disorderly,
would have been supposed to be trying to *undo* all the
good work of parents and teachers, and to set children
against lawful authority. Now, everybody knows
that the very business of the Gymnast is to undo the
cramping effect of the positions rendered necessary by
the exigencies of study and of society; and nobody
objects to its being done. We have all found out that
the Gymnasts are the friends, not the enemies, of Order.
We have seen the beneficial effects of gymnastic on the
pupils; few notice the silent influence for good which it
has exerted, through the pupils, on the parents and
teachers; but it *has* exerted an influence on us all.
What mother could condemn her daughter's desire for
reversal of physical position as "unseemly" and "unladylike," in the face of the fact that the girl will presently
assume the condemned posture by the orders of the
graceful lady who presides in the Gymnasium? We
are content, now, to tell little girls that standing with
one's hand on one's hip is a proceeding more suited to
the play-room than the drawing-room. The Gymnasts
only profess to cure the weakness of children's muscles;
in reality they are helping to eradicate the irreverent

dogmatism of parents.   Let Logos-teachers boldly claim
the right to do for children's minds what the Gymnast
does for their bodies, *i.e.*, renew vital elasticity by
periodic *reversal of attitude*, and after a time the public
will grow accustomed to the idea that it is some teachers'
business to do *nothing*, except vitalize the minds of
children by undoing other people's teaching.   The
conceit of specialist teachers of all sorts will have to give
way before the Logical equation of brain-rhythm, as
the conceit of would-be-genteel Mammas has had to give
way before the Logic of muscular exercise.   And we
cannot lay too much stress on this point : the Gymnast
is an absolute Nihilist ; he does *Nothing*—except *reverse
the positions of the muscles ;* he has no results to show,
except increased health and strength.   The Logos or
Pulsation-doctrine, pure and holy as it is, may, in one
sense, be described as the Scavenger of our life.   By
burning up all that is specious and false, it prevents the
development of those abnormal conditions which to the
ignorant seem like culture, but which are in reality the
product of corruption, the source of disease, and the
main cause of insanity.

Those who, of old, attempted to base National Education on the principle of the *Logos*, or rhythmic pulsation,
struck the true key-note at starting.   The symbol of the
covenant made with man by Infinite Knowledge was the
Rainbow ; which no man can capture or embalm or
enshrine ; which is made by the breaking up of the One
Light into many colours, to fade before long into the
Unity of white light again ; and leaves nowhere in all
the world a trace of its ever having existed, except in
Man's heart an impression of spiritual beauty, and in his

mind a suggestion how to discover the Laws of Light.
The type of mind which asks "*Cui bono?*" of every
lesson for which there is nothing to show at Examination is the same as the type of mind which sneers
because the Sacred Ark of the Hebrew Covenant contains, practically, NOTHING—a few old-world tales
illustrative of a state of society long passed away; a few
self-evident laws of morality; and a mass of rules, very
uninteresting, and to a large extent negative in form,
tedious to carry out, of no obvious utility, but, on the
contrary, in themselves a hindrance to active life. Of
positive information, *Nothing.*   It is time that teachers
at least should be taught to understand that, though
man has a right to desire and procure whatever he wants,
the inner shrine whence Truth issues to hold converse
with man may not be desecrated by the presence of
immediately realizable results. If it be so desecrated,
the Blessed Guest departs. In that Ark is preserved
what the Rainbow leaves behind when it fades into white
light:—the Keys of the Infinite Store-house of Science;
the canons of the Art of Thinking; the Secret of the
Method whereby man may draw down Truth from
Heaven, without blighting either his body or his soul.
Life lives in that empty Ark; the true life of man's
brain. For we are the children of the Creator; not His
mere handiwork, made arbitrarily, unlike Himself; but
the outcome of His very thought-processes; and sanity,
for us, means thinking as He thinks, so far as we think
at all. And (if His work reveals His manner of thinking) He thinks in an incessant rhythmic pulsation of
alternate "positing and denying," of constructing and
sweeping away; a pulsation which produces the *appear-*

ance of negation and the *reality* of power. It is in vain
that we try to fight against, or to ignore, this rhythmic
alternation of contrary notions. If we carefully embody
it in our daily study, it becomes to us a source of constant power, like the movement of our lungs. If we
forget it, it never forgets to sweep our work away.
Unless it has helped to build the mind, their labour is
but lost that built it. It is vain that we haste to rise
early, and late take rest, and devour many carefully
compiled text-books; to those who love the Invisible,
Formless, alternate-beating Unity, the knowledge which
is power comes even during sleep.[1]

CHAPTER XX

TRINITY MYTHS

"Holy, Holy, Holy, Lord God of Hosts."

In very old times, wise men devised a special method
for counteracting the dangers of specialization, a standard
test by which a student could judge whether his mode
of recuperation was suited to the nature of his special
dangers. Their method rested on a perception of the
fact that man is so organized as to perceive the Divine
in three principal modes :—

    1. By the study of Nature, of the work of Creation,
the most interesting part of which, to early peoples, was
the observation of the Starry Heavens. God, *as Creator*,
was called by Indians *Brahma*, by Semitic peoples
Elohim, by Christians *God the Father*.

[1] "The Creed of Sanity."

2. God is revealed as a *Race-Preserver ;* in the dividing of the animal Creation by lines across which union is infertile, and by other lines across which union is unhealthy; and also, and chiefly, in the singular differences introduced into the human body by diversities of culture, of climate, and of circumstance; and in the danger of too sudden interruptions of ancestral habit. God as *Race-Preserver* was called by the Indians *Vishnu ;* and in each country by some name special to itself. The idea of the *Race Preserver* is embodied in the name *God of Israël* (and perhaps also in *Jehovah ;* said by some to be the tribal God of the pre-Mosaic Hebrews).

3. Persons of sensitive temperament and introspective habits recognize the fact of an actual contact between their souls and the Divine, of a personal inspiration of truth which comes to them in some manner not explicable by reference either to impressions on the senses or to intellectual conclusions. And, as any deep sorrow or strong affection increases the capacity for receiving this poetic inspiration, and as it is often increased also by severe physical suffering, God, as inspirer, was thought of as *The Purifier by the Fire of Love and Pain ;* called by the Indians *Siva.* This idea is represented by the Jewish word *Adonai*, and by the " Holy Spirit " of our churches.

The Philosophers perceived that terrible dangers were caused by the divided and over-specialized study of Divine action. The worshippers of Brahma, the Creator, lapse into a cold and immoral contemplation of Nature. Nature contains not only beauty, but also what in man would be cruelties and lust; and those who think of God *only* as Creator, too often become indifferent to moral order in human life.   Moreover, as Nature has many aspects, each branch of Science tends to represent the Creator differently.   To the imagination of the mere Geometrician, the infinite means infinite space; to the student of meteoric phenomena, the infinite is represented by mere force; to the arithmetician by mere number. To those of old who specially valued physical strength, God was a Bull; to those who specially valued cunning, a Serpent.

On the other hand, Vishnu, the Race-Preserver, comes to be thought of too much as the preserver of one's own tribe.   Each tribe comes to have its own preserver, who fights against the preservers of other tribes.   As patriotism degenerates into tyranny over other nations, so religious gratitude for the preservation of one's own race degenerates into contempt for the divine preservers of other races.

But the worst transformation is that which falls on the idea of the *inspirer who teaches by the fire of love. Purification by fire* degenerates into *destruction by fire.* The inspirer by *love and pain* becomes *Siva the Destroyer,* and then *Moloch,* who claims as his offering the burning alive of innocent babies.   It is found, too, that pain is not the only condition under which the faculty for receiving poetic inspiration is momentarily increased; pleasure also heightens it.   Inspiration of a certain sort can be got up by wine; Siva the Inspirer is thought of as Bacchus the wine-god, who is gratified by drunken orgies.   The Adonai-idea degenerates into Adonis, the god of beauty of form, and into Aphrodite, the goddess of grace; finally into Cupid, the god of light love-fancies, and Venus the goddess of vicious indulgence.

And the worst thing about all these horrible fables was that they embodied a certain truth ; and the attempt to disprove them was futile. Gentile philosophers were driven to distraction by the impossibility of making men disbelieve things which, though so pernicious, were somehow true to human experience.

Down into all this ghastly tangle of great truths and hideous faslehoods came the mighty reformers who organised the Trinity-doctrine. After an exhaustive and masterly study of the process by which good degenerates into evil, they discovered that falsehood comes by the dividedness of truth, and that the unification of all aspects of deity would infallibly purify each. It is hardly too bold a metaphor, if we say that, by the law of the Trinity, the various aspects of deity are to be prevented from slipping down-hill in various directions, by firmly linking them together at the top. The Hebrew Scriptures contain a record of canons, which, if observed, would set philosophy free to develop indefinitely, by forever preventing it from degenerating into debauch or folly.

These canons are binding as long as Judaism or Humanity lasts, being founded on the nature of the human mind. Jesus, when accused of disregarding the law of Moses (because he had taken upon himself to neglect a few minutiæ of the technical rules, which he considered interfered with his usefulness), truly replied that heaven and earth must pass away before one jot or tittle of the law should fail.

By the Law of Israël, each aspect or facet of the God-idea is to be clearly presented in its purity.

1. All Creative energies are summed up in the one

word Elohim.   There is to be no God of Light distinct from the God of darkness; no devil who causes evil contrasted with the deity who gives good; no bull-god or serpent-god, no god of thunder, or god of wind; all natural science is one, and is the worship of Elohim.

2. Homage is to be paid to the Race-Preserver, not by prejudices against other virtuous and pious tribes, but by abstaining, in His honour, from unnatural mixtures and infertile unions.   While He is to be worshipped by Jews as the "God of Israël," they are to remember that He cares equally for all the tribes of the earth.   The preservation of law and order is not to be a mere cunning device for securing the supremacy of one's own tribe, but a perpetual worship of Jehovah, the God of all the races.

3. But especially is danger from divided and partial worships to be avoided in the direction of the *search after inspiration.*   No devices are to be resorted to, to heighten the *sensation* of inspiration.   Jews are to put themselves *en rapport* with the Inspirer, only so far as a holy life will attain that end.   Not passion or intoxication, but solemnity and abstinence, are to characterize their attempts to approach personally to Adonai. Sacrifices are to be made to Him by fire, in his character of *Purifier by Fire;* but none of these exhibit any other connection with pain or death than is shown by learning to kill animals for food in the least hardening and most merciful manner possible.   Jews are to inflict no needless suffering, either on themselves or on other creatures, for their own excitement or amusement. Adonai is neither Moloch, the pain-giver, nor Adonis, the lust-exciter; but the Inspirer who purifies by love.

But pure and holy as are each of these aspects of deity in the Mosaic conception, still no race could be trusted to preserve them in their purity, unless they were seen to be different aspects of one eternal fact. Hear, O Israël, the deliverer from bondage is *One*. The same idea is expressed in a lovely old lullaby hymn, in which, five times over, the name *Saviour* is given to the grouping of the three attributes, "Elohim," "Adonai," and "King" (or Orderer, or Organizer). By some Christian theologians, strange to say, not only are the three aspects of the God-idea made into three individuals,[1] three real personalities, but one of these personalities alone is considered to be the *Saviour;* and that one was manifested in human shape to avert the wrath of another.

Nothing, however, could be clearer than that each of the three principal facets of the God-idea is distinctly traceable in the Hebrew Scriptures; and Jewish theologians might gracefully make the admission that, in that respect, Christians have seen something in their sacred books which most of themselves have missed. But, though individual rabbis may have failed to detect the use made in the Pentateuch of the old Trinity-Myth, the Synagogue ritual still enshrines it. Not only is the triple Kadosh a recognition of the threefoldness of religious emotion; but each aspect of the God-idea receives its special and appropriate greeting. It would be impossible to convey to Jews, accustomed from infancy to their worship, any notion of the impression made on a Christian visitor by the difference in the tone of the three strains interwoven in it:—The homage of

[1] *Persona* means a mask, not an individual.

astronomers to the Creator in the greetings at New Year and new Moon; the homage to the Race-Preserver, God of Abraham, Isaac, and Jacob; the homage to the Eternal Reign of Love the Inspirer, in the oft-recurring anthem: "Adonai reigneth, Adonai hath reigned, Adonai shall reign for ever and ever."

That the startling effect of these three elements of Jewish worship, so contrasted and yet so exquisitely blended, should have driven Christian theologians out of their senses, and into mad raptures of delight and wonder, is intelligible. That they should, in consequence, have written much caressing rhapsody, more poetic than accurate, about the Jewish Scriptures, is pardonable; there are occasions on which it is not to one's credit to be able to keep quite prosaically sane; and one's first contact with the Hebrew religion is one of those occasions. But the *creed of Israël* is very evidently a caution to avoid the horrible dangers into which the heathen fell by dividing the different facets of divine influence; and the statement that Moses meant Jews to worship more than one Person, passes the legitimate limits of even poetic license.

The true use of the Trinity-doctrine is as a standard whereby to judge whether we are really getting for our own minds the vitalizing influence of the Unity-doctrine. Whatever facet of the God-idea is presented to us by our studies, we should be careful to remember the other aspects when we are preparing for repose. We should remember the essential Unity between the three facets; a Unity such that we cannot keep our minds in a condition to do justice to our own special subject, unless we pay reverence to all three aspects of the Divine when we are preparing ourselves for rest. In this Trinity none is afore or after other, none is greater or less than another; but the whole three are co-eternal and co-equal; and he that will be safe must think after this model. So says that marvellous old Credo, in which, in a degenerate age, well-meaning idolaters enshrined the remnants of an older Philosophy which seemed about to die out.

The Law of Moses is holy as of old, and whoever speaks of it should do so with reverence. Those who disregard it, do just as truly lapse into idolatry as men did three thousand years ago. The mere mathematician conceives of a Space or a Number; his absorption in the contemplation of which deadens his interest in other forms of truth. The man who deifies natural science often sinks into a mere vivisectionist, who inflicts torture at random, for the gratification of an idle freak of curiosity.

Adonai has his dangers too. Spiritualism and æstheticism each has its own vicious modes of heightening the sense of inspiration. The Catholic worship of Jesus and Mary, by nuns and monks respectively, often degenerates into the worship of Adonis and Aphrodite, under other names; and has sometimes all the more distracting effect on the imagination, for being, nowadays, prevented by conventual regulations from exhaling itself in physical scandals; and the Moloch-form of fire-worship still exists in the belief in an *everlasting* and *non-purifying* hell.

As for the second facet or division of the God-idea, Vishnu, how much better would have been the influence of Christian Missionaries had they not sanctioned the heathenish notion that God has given no truth except

to European races! They are as essentially worshippers
of a tribal God as the savages whom they would convert.

Nor are Jews guiltless of this form of idolatry. No
Bismarck or Stoecker could stir up epidemics of anti-
Semitism, were the Jews, who fidget over little details
of rule, equally true to the essential canons of their
faith! The way in which too many Jews trust to
"Jehovah" to protect them from the natural consequence
of their own actions, is as idolatrous and heathenish as
is the trust of a Catholic peasant that his own special
saint will keep his family in health, while he neglects
common precautions of hygiene and morality. The
"God of Israël" which many Jews worship is essentially
an eidolon or image of character evolved within the
Jewish mind. Some entirely ignore that Jehovah is
race-preserver of other races, and that therefore all knowledge of hygienic rules discovered by Gentiles should
form part of the religion of Jews. They neglect to
worship God as Elohim or Creator, therefore they despise
the marvellous new knowledge which He is pouring out,
about the effect of the lower creatures on man, and of
human beings on each other. And when trouble comes
to them, in consequence of such ignorance, if any preacher
speak to them of God as *Adonai, the purifier by suffering,
the inspirer by love*, they turn away either in anger or in
contempt. Thus they make of themselves what in
medical language is called a "foreign body" in the
general commonwealth; and their private virtues, and
family piety, and loyalty to the tribal God of Israël are
unavailing to prevent their being felt to be a danger to
the State.

Idolatry, therefore, is not at an end in Europe, among

either Jews or Gentiles. Nor is the need for seeking
the cure of social ills in the worship of the great Unity
less than it was when Israël came out of Egypt. If we
were not idolaters, the educationists who are imposing
their cruel laws on all types of children alike, would
remember that the Law-maker is also a Race-Preserver,
and forbids a too rapid change of ancestral habits; the
Salvation Army would believe that salvation means, not
hysteric tension on one aspect of deity, but reverence
for all aspects of that divine Creator, whose laws include
a law of reaction after violent nervous action, and a law
of hereditary recoil of posterity from the exaggerations
of a preceding generation; sensitive and "mediumistic"
women would be trained in the knowledge of the orderly
Elohim revealed by Science; our luxurious æsthetes
who worship Adonis, the Art-Inspirer, will remember
that the true Adonai will sooner or later purify all by
the fire of pain; thus force would be stored up for the
solution of our practical problems, which now is being
wasted in the struggle to gain that which cannot satisfy.
The wisdom Who came out of Egypt with Moses still
cries to us, though few hear her voice: " Hear, O Israël,
and hear, O Man; divided Gods make us slaves; the
Deliverer from Bondage is Unity."

And every man, when he is about to prepare for rest
by worshipping The Inconceivable Unity, should remember that the true God is not a mere reflection of his
own personal predilections, but is equally Holy in each
of the three aspects under which He reveals Himself to
Humanity.

Another form of the Trinity-doctrine is the *time-
division*, past, present, and future. This time-trinity is

just touched on in both Hebrew and Christian ritual. Its essence is preserved in the myth of the three Fates, called in the Odin-Legends Urda, Verdendi, and Skelda ; or *Was*, *Is-Becoming*, and *Shall-Be*.   The student who takes an equal interest in the History of the Past, the development of the Present, and the destinies of the Future, keeps his mind balanced.   If any one of them be neglected, the fates become furies who avenge ; or Vampires who suck away the student's life-blood and make of him an evil fate to other men.   If the balance is duly kept by remembering all three equally in religious meditation, the three Fates become three Graces.

This dual aspect of the three Fates is made more intelligible by reference to the dual form of the Legend of the Birds who feed Seers with wisdom.   These birds are now doves, now ravens.   They inspire peaceful doctrines, or prompt to deeds of darkness and cruelty, according as the Prophet does, or does not, unify their several inspirations.   The true Prophet is *he to whose head both birds come.*

CHAPTER XXI

STUDY OF ANTAGONISTIC THINKERS

"Audi Alteram Partem."

WHENEVER a Law of Nature is ignored, it asserts itself as a destructive agent.   The remedy is not to rail at the Law, but to study it and enlist its action into our service.   The savage prays his Manitou not to send storms ; the civilized man puts up a lightning-conductor to his house, and he who knows how to do this, knows also how to use electricity for the purpose of advancing civilization still further. Parents are often distressed at facts which mean that the young mind is violently impelled to satisfy the Law of alternate action, by throwing itself under the influence of some teacher whose views are opposed to those of former teachers. What the young mind imperatively needs is not conflict of opinion but alternation of attitude and of emotion; we should try so to organize life that this relief can be found without actual contradiction. Young people need contact with persons who *feel* differently from their parents; teachers might give that relief without suggesting that the parents are mistaken or wrong. But at present there is so much tension on questions of opinion that, if parents select teachers whose tendencies are opposite to their own, the children learn from the strangers to think their parents mistaken; whereas the parent who seeks out for his children influences counter to his own, gives thereby the best possible proof of being in the right; for he proves that he has more confidence in the Eternal Truth of the Principle of alternation than in his own special opinions.

All who live in the intimacy of great original thinkers, observe how incompetent the families and intimate friends of such men usually are to understand them. The reason, I believe, is that men of Genius attract so much attention as to destroy the mental elasticity of those around them, and thus weaken their mental vigour. The son of a great thinker does not acquire true vigour till he throws himself out of his father's sphere of influence. The psychology of the matter not being understood, the thinker thus loses the aid of those who, by their very heredity, should be best able to help him.

Long observations of the families and followers of original thinkers, and some experience as a secretary to several such, have led me to form a plan for myself which I find so useful that I venture to recommend it to the notice of the children, pupils, and secretaries of men of Genius.

When I find my power of understanding my employer coming to an end, and myself growing weary of his peculiar style, I try to find out to whom, among those on his own intellectual level, he personally feels most antagonistic and is most unjust. I give myself a *bath* (so to speak) in the ideas of this rival, and (if opportunity serves) in his actual personal influence. For instance, supposing that I were working under Mr. Spurgeon, the famous preacher, and grew tired, I should seek Mr. Bradlaugh.[1] I should seek, not conflict of opinion, but variety of attitude and emotion. I should not ask him what he thought of the Millennium, nor talk to him about Mr. Spurgeon; but I should try to get, somehow, a bath in Mr. Bradlaugh's peculiar *magnetism*. I should ask him to go to an Oratorio with me; and try to get him to talk to me about the Future destinies of Man. When the needful relaxation had been produced, this (to judge from all my experience) is what would happen:—I should find myself writing, without effort or fatigue, an Article on the Future of Humanity, of which Mr. Spurgeon (and perhaps also Mr. Bradlaugh) would say: "You have expressed my meaning more exactly than I

---

[1] I mention these two gentlemen because, as I have never studied under either of them, nothing I say can be taken as personal.

could do it; you have said what I have been trying to say but could not express satisfactorily."

A little tact and a little explanation are needed to induce even a Philosopher to understand why his secretary or follower wants the relief of being counter-magnetized by his bitterest opponent. But the result being that one is better able to help each philosopher, it is to be hoped that learned men will, before long, grow accustomed to the idea; and gradually induce parents and teachers to generate brain-force in young people by a similar unexhausting method.

CHAPTER XXII

OUR RELATION TO THE SACRED TRIBE

"Israël was despised and rejected; when we see him there is no beauty
  that we should desire him. He is full of sorrows and acquainted with
  grief. We hid our faces from him; he was despised and we esteemed
  him not.

"We thought him stricken of God; but he was wounded for our trans-
  gressions, and with his stripes we are healed.

"He shall see of the travail of his soul and shall be satisfied; by his
  knowledge shall he justify many; for he makes intercession for trans-
  gressors."

THE Path of intellectual Progress is a Pulsation between the active study of Nature's variety of manifestations and repose in the contemplation of The Unmanifested Unity. Science and Art tend to become, every now and then, entangled in and weakened by the overwhelming multiplicity of sensible facts. But Nature has provided us with a Sacred Tribe, subjected from Time immemorial to a peculiar discipline, which somewhat unfits its members to be great Leaders in the sensuous Arts, because it gives to them a strong tendency to think of The Unseen Unity. The effect of this Tribe on the thought-life of the world is very like what was described in Chapter XIX. as the effect of the true Logos-teacher on a School; when Science has exhausted itself and wandered off into too much detail, some Jew like Mendelssohn or Spinoza, or some Gentile who has been saturating his soul in Jewish lore, like Gratry or Boole, prepares for true recuperative repose by striking afresh the key-note of Sabbath, the Name of The Invisible Unity. For reasons which were pointed out in Chapter XIX., he who does this seems to be out of the line of progress, because he ignores and neutralizes much which others have been doing and which seems essential. But when once we have realized that nothing is more essential to progress than strong pulsation we shall lose the feeling that the peculiarly Jewish type of mind is out of tune with true refinement; we shall turn to it for the repose which gives new energy to all forms of culture.

The function of Judaism is perhaps best understood when we remember that the early Christian asceticism was not an isolated phenomenon, but a typical specimen of a group of facts, the natural outcome of tendencies whose action is essential to our intellectual life, but whose uncontrolled action would destroy society. Of these tendencies, Judaism is the corrective and controller.

In order to avoid entering into disputed questions of theology, let us look at the action of these tendencies as exhibited on a small scale in our own day.

James Hinton wrote a charming little book called *The Mystery of Pain*, wherein he announced that failure and suffering are the greatest boons that life has to offer. This and his other published works were hailed by many as a new Gospel. He next proceeded to state, in conversations and in private lectures, that "Heaven looks down on no sight so cursed as a happy home;" because, he said, in order to keep home happy, men ignore the claims of strangers. Finally, he propounded certain theories of sublime self-abnegation, which have, in one way or another, been the ruin of nearly all who paid any attention to them.

The career of such men becomes more intelligible, when one knows that James Hinton habitually went out in winter insufficiently clad, not in order to give his great-coat to a beggar, but to give himself the pleasure of suffering from cold. James Hinton would have been a useful subordinate in any well-organized school of Philosophy; unfortunately we have in England no well-organized Schools; and a large circle set Hinton up, for a time, as Leader. Now when a community has arrived at such a condition that men can be set up as thought-leaders who are born without the healthy appetite for self-preservation which is the necessary physical basis of all knowledge of the means by which society is preserved, that community needs to be taken in hand and controlled by the influence (one might almost say, by the magnetism) of a morally sane race. In ordinary times, Judaism keeps itself in the background, and leaves Gentile thought to develop in its own way. But when Philosophy has evaporated into the fourth dimension, when it has played with the Eternal till it has shrivelled out of itself the perception alike of locality and of epoch, of possibility and of sequence, of perspective and of proportion,

then is a fitting occasion for Judaism to come to the
front.   It reminds us that He Who gave to us a certain
limited power of sympathy with strangers, reserved for
Himself the luxury of limitless sympathy, precisely
because He is not a stranger but the Father of us all;
that this Father in Heaven has placed us on earth; that
the particular stratum of the fourth dimension wherein
He has located us is that of three dimensional (*i.e.*,
physical) consciousness;   that mere vague sensuous
sympathy, not safeguarded by Law, may be not virtue
but vice; and that the Eternal, acting within the limits
of His own Holiness, has imposed on our faculties an
order in development and a sequence of action which
cannot be safely ignored.

   We are prone to think Jews indifferent to religion
and careless of our well-being, because they leave us so
much to ourselves.   Our own restless fussiness causes
us to think every one callous who is not incessantly
fidgeting about, trying to improve and convert somebody else.   The New Testament (to say nothing of the
Old) might have taught us that he is the best teacher
who most perfectly reflects the Divine patience and
willingness to *suspend action*.   The Ideal Saviour seems
to be asleep, leaving others to manage the ship as they
will; till they cry to him in the storm, " Master, we
perish." [1]   In another version of the storm-myth,[2] the
teacher, perceiving that men would make him a
King by force, retires to commune with his God, and
leaves the disciples to go on their way alone.   But
when it is dark and the tempest arises, they find that,
without using their means of transport, he has reached

------

[1] Luke viii.   [2] John vi.

the same spot as themselves. When the need is sorest he is found at hand, saying: " I am here; be not afraid."

James Hinton was well aware of his own lack of stability, and dreaded above all things being set up as an intellectual Pope. His own instinct told him that the true path of progress consists in incessant pulsation between the strong and the mobile types of mind. He often illustrated the relation between the two types by the following Parable. Little boys and girls, he said, play together indiscriminately, regardless of sex; and all copy the eldest or cleverest child. But as soon as that mental difference begins to appear which is to end in a possibility of fuller sympathy, it is often marked by a mutual repulsion, which lasts till the time for mutual understanding has come. The girls call the boys " Horrid, noisy, greedy, vulgar creatures, who don't care for fairy-tales and who destroy the dolls"; and the boys call the girls " Silly, sentimental molly-coddles, who can't understand anything sensible." Each side has a perfect right to its own opinion ; and, should the quarrels become too violent, it is not of much use to preach solemnly about the sinfulness of lack of charity ; it is better to remind all parties that when they are older they will feel differently; and to encourage them, in the meantime, to assist in each other's education. Nor is it wise to put too much check on the natural repulsion, by forcibly assimilating the lives of boys and girls; those young people are found ultimately of most use to each other in whom the differentiation of character has been allowed to develop.

This illustration surely throws light on the whole relation between Jews and Aryans. People who hope to improve the world, either by converting Jews to religions cast in the Trinitarian mould, or by depriving us of the adjuncts to faith which it is natural for us to seek, belong essentially to the same order of reasoners as those who fancy that boys are made more refined by being taught to pose in effeminate attitudes, or girls more logical by being forbidden to do fancy-embroidery. Those turn out best-bred who respect the individuality on each side, and yet are willing to learn from each other. The old fable of Narcissus tells the fate of those who can love nothing but the reflection of themselves.

The stern spiritual discipline which has made Jews indifferent to much which we think essential to religion, the sentimental and somewhat hysterical weakness which characterizes Aryan pietism, are among the means by which the differentiation is being effected ; while sufficient proof that it is still incomplete is afforded by the fact that misunderstandings still arise. And perhaps no antagonism could prove ultimately to have been so great a misfortune, as would be the arresting of the differentiation before it is complete. Europe is quarrelling with imperfectly developed Jews ; but it long ago lost its heart to the typical Jew, as seen in Vision, though as yet it knows not what it was that it saw. Christ, as he exists in Christian tradition, is not so much the historical Jesus as personified Judaism. The simple manliness of Jewish piety has so dazzled us, that we have invented a whole system of theology to account for its difference from our own more effeminate graces. Underlying all forms of Christian doctrine, there is the deep human truth that Gentile thought, with its Art and its fancy, its sensibility and its weakness, is the "Bride of Christ,"—the counterpart and destined helpmeet of the pure strong Hebrew faith. We Christians have got our life into confusion by trying to copy our Ideal "Christ"; we are not enough like him to know how to set about it. Jews do not go into ecstacies about "Jesus," because they are (potentially at least) himself.[1]   When Judaism and Christianity have discovered their true relation to each other; when we Christians, especially, have realized that our true function is not so much copying Christ ourselves as organizing social life so as to facilitate the development of Judaism into its natural likeness to him, surely that will be the Millennium prophesied of old, "the Bridal of the Earth and Sky."

This may seem a romantic way of dealing with those epidemics of Jew-hating, which, as a prosaic matter of fact, often originate in trade jealousies and in envy of the special business faculty of Jews. The true Prophet, however, is not he who conjures himself into mystic trances, in order that by shutting his eyes to earth he may see into Heaven; but he who looks at the facts that God shows on earth by the Light which God sends from Heaven. Such an one can algebraize the slightest indications of progressive tendency in man. He thrills with the joy of future harvests when he sees one plant become more fruitful under human care; and hears all Handel's music in the tones of Jubal's lyre. And if it

---

[1] I speak here only of Jewish reformers in religion. Of the Jews who devote themselves to Finance, Commerce and Politics I have nothing to say, except that they are what Europe has made of them. What Europe *has* made of them should be carefully studied by those who are undertaking the task of bringing Chinese and Hindus into contact with Western civilization.

be vouchsafed to him to realize something of the true relation between the Aryan and the Jew, he knows henceforth the meaning of Isaiah's golden dreams. Those who are weak and contemptible while severed, become sublime and strong when united. " Il y a au monde une chose sainte et sublime ; c'est l'union de deux êtres imparfaits.   On est souvent trompé, souvent blessé, et souvent malheureux ; mais on aime ; et quand on est sur le bord de la tombe, on dit :—J'ai aimé ; c'est moi qui ai vécu, et non pas un être factice créé par mon orgueil et mon ennui."

This truth we all know.   It lies deep down in all our hearts.   We Gentiles know it, but are powerless to carry our knowledge into action ; for impatience clouds our perceptions, and we lose Love by premature unifications.   The unregulated indulgence of impulses of Altruism destroys nerve-stamina ; and, as a consequence, we find mere unreasoning dislikes stronger than our faith in the Eternal Principle of Love.   Jews have been taught, and will at length teach us, that the Love which is stronger than death and which survives the grave is not to be snatched at by any emotional passion, whether religious or poetic ; it is brought into our lives by in all things awaiting the due time, and by the systematic consecration of natural duty.

CHAPTER XXIII

PROGRESS, FALSE AND TRUE

"The Wind bloweth as it listeth; and thou canst not tell whence it cometh or whither it goeth."

IT may seem to some readers anomalous to write the words False Progress. It seems to be often ignored that any such thing can exist. Many suppose that so long as we are moving, we are necessarily moving onwards. Others again suppose that movement is of no use unless it be in the ultimately true direction; they forget that turmoil, which is useless for progress, may be useful in preventing stagnation.

Nothing is more certain than that some Power beyond our ken forces us to go through a great deal of false Progress, *i.e.* of motion, the tendency of which is not in the direction towards which Humanity is really tending. We are constantly deceived in this matter. We think we are making a progressive movement, and all the while we may have been retrograding towards barbarism, or making a rapid rush off on a path which we shall have to retrace before we can rejoin the onward March of Humanity. We have to discount our jubilation about progress; we certainly progress on the whole; but we are, at any given moment, liable to mistake for progress something which is in reality the reverse.

When the Prophets saw, as we see every summer day, how the wind catches up the particles of dust and carries them along, whirling them round and round as it goes, they felt that progress carries mankind on so; not in one straight line, but round and round, yet steadily moving on all the while.   The same direction which is really in the march of progress at one moment, is a mere flying out of it, off at a tangent, at another.   That is why fashion is not progress.   Fashion is mere imitation. Now if we watch the wind-storm, we see that to go East to-day may be real progress, but to go East to-morrow because some one else went East yesterday may be not progress but a departure from it.   All the outer life of the world, political, educational, social, philosophic, moves onward by incessant change of direction.   There is no real misfortune in this; we should miss much that is valuable if we restricted ourselves to going always in one direction.   The danger is that if we have no standard of right direction, we may lose our way altogether, and fly off into isolation. Therefore, just in the middle of the whirl, Providence has placed one thing which moves on in a steady sweep towards the ultimate Truth, and which was never meant to take any part in the whirling movement to which all else is subject.   And that one thing is the religion of Israël.   It stands always in the centre of the world's march, as a test of the right direction.   Nothing is going far wrong which keeps, as it were, well within sight of that standard.   And when we have gone a little way wrong, it acts as a test to help us to find our way back to the right path.   Judaism helps the world to judge of its own direction.   This standard is not so rigid as to make all people alike; it leaves us all free to differ in detail; it allows Gentiles to try experiments and to gain the experience that can only be acquired by making mistakes and then correcting them; but if we take heed to the legacy left us by the old Prophets, it enables us to avoid drifting dangerously far from the right road. If people were discussing which is East and which is West, and one happened to catch sight of the sun rising, he would listen to no further discussion ; he would *know* which was East. And if people are discussing what is true and what is false progress, and one of them discovers that the road he is going is leading to a clearer understanding of the religion of Israël, that man has *seen* the Orient.

Suppose that the thought-life of an age or a Nation has diverged from the march of Humanity, and its philosophers cannot agree among themselves which is the path back towards the line of true progress. One says, "This is the way ;" and another says, "No, it is that ;" and a third obstinately wants to persevere in the road he is going along. But if one of them catches sight of the old religion of Israël, if he finds himself saying, "*Now* I understand the nature of the Law which the old Psalmists loved ; *now* I know for what the martyrs of Israël gave up their lives, and what gave them courage," that man is troubled with no more doubts. He argues no more. He lets other men go on in their own road, quite certain that he is on the right track at last, and that those who are turning their backs on that beacon are going away from true Progress.

Perhaps the difficulty of distinguishing true progress from false is never so great as in what relates to mental cultivation, to refinement, to Education. It is here that the admission of Jews or other persons of Asiatic origin into European schools becomes most valuable as a test. If I had to select a school for a Christian girl, the first question I should ask would be, not how many pupils

passed the Higher Examinations (for no Examination
is any security against flashy and unreal modes of thinking); I should ask, first, whether the Jewesses who
attend the school improve or deteriorate by being there;
whether they are found to be, on the whole, a good or a
bad influence.   Every country and every school gets, as
some French writer has said, *the Jews which it deserves.*
A school or a country where Jews are found to be a
deteriorating influence is one where public opinion is
judging of progress by a false standard.

So it is on a larger scale.   A Nation may seem to be
rushing onward in a line which is supposed to be that of
culture; but if it turns out that the Asiatics who take
part in that culture drift out of sight of their own
religion, if they lose their perception of the meaning of
their own past, they are leaving the line of true progress;
and whoever is sharing the same kind of education is
leaving it along with them.   Whatever culture produces
that effect on Asiatics is deadening and stupefying for
all parties ; it may look like improvement, but it par-
takes of the nature of white paint over corruption.   It
will end by leading all parties towards impiety and
vulgarity—the Asiatics first, of course; but ultimately
everybody else as well.   But if Asiatics can throw themselves heartily into the culture of a country without
losing hold of their own religions, we may be sure that
that culture is founded on something approximately like
the true laws of human development.   If the result of
successive changes in an Educational code is that Asiatics
can make excursions into the Science, the Literature,
the Philosophy of their age, and come easily back, with
fresh energy and fresh clearness, to the work of advancing

their own religion, then the rest of us may feel assured that we are not being led far wrong; for whatever movement brought about that result must have been a movement towards the line of true Progress.[1]

CHAPTER XXIV

THE MESSIANIC KINGDOM

" It is a slight thing that thou shouldest restore Israël ; I will set thee for a Light to the Gentiles."—ISAIAH xlix. 6.

THE words " Exodus " and " Reform " have a natural and vital connection ; the founders of the Mosaic system intended to prepare a standing council of *reformers*, a body capable of quietly reforming all the thought-material of the world, by introducing into intellectual life that rhythmic motion which is characteristic of physical life.

The true Re-former is distinguished not by any particular opinions or practices, but by a something, impossible to define, the very presence of which makes stagnant thought *uncomfortable*. He possesses faculties which orthodoxy lacks ; he has intuitions the source of which is unknown to it, the purpose and meaning of which it fails to conceive, and about which it only understands, vaguely, that they threaten danger to its stability and peace. When the young Mazzini was thrown, innocent, into prison, officialism gave this account of the motives for his arrest :—

" *He is a young man of remarkable talent; very fond of*

[1] Given as a lecture at the Jewish Working-Men's Club, London.

solitary walks by night; and habitually silent about his meditations. The government does not like young men of talent the subject of whose meditations is unknown to it."

The instinct of the Austrian government had discovered that when Genius goes forth alone to listen to the Voices of Nature, events are likely to occur soon afterwards calculated to disturb the peace of stagnation. And, as usual, tyranny forgot to inquire whether imprisoning Genius is likely to cure it of a taste for liberty!

Just so, tyranny has, on many occasions, forgotten to inquire whether trying to cramp the Theistic Seer-hood of Judaism is likely to cure it of the habit of seeing God.

The function of Reform has hitherto been carried on for the Gentile world, episodically and violently, by a succession of such men as Savonarola, Bruno, Luther, Cromwell, Wesley, Mazzini, Maurice, Renan and Hinton. The intention of the founders of Mosaism was to organize a body which should (after some centuries of preliminary discipline) acquire the power of accustoming the whole world to having that function performed for it as regularly, quietly and constantly as the lungs reform the blood.

Judaism, *as a sect*, far from becoming more intelligible and more tolerated because of the progress of liberality and culture, must, on the contrary, become more impossible and more intolerable with every advance in civilization. It has no place in the modern world, unless it is the intellectual heart-and-lungs of Humanity, viz., an organ whose function is to receive all the thought-material gathered by the Gentile world; purify and aërate it by submitting it to the action of that circulating rhythm which is characteristic of Nature's vital processes and of the Jewish discipline; and give it back to Gentiles in the form of pure religion. Humanity can become an organic body only when its circulatory apparatus becomes well established.

The possibility of performing the true function of the Reformer does not depend on any particular opinion about the Bible, or any other book. Nor does it depend on either following or abjuring any given mode of conducting ritual, nor on the possession of any special item of knowledge. No persons ever performed that function more efficiently than did the compilers of the Pentateuch (whoever they may have been); in their day there was no Bible, either to believe or to disbelieve. Jesus performed it; and if any fact is known about him, it is that he took the ritual just as he found it; conforming to established custom whenever his doing so did not interfere with honesty or charity, and laying no great stress on any details. Moses Mendelssohn may be said to have been actually the heart and lungs of the Berlin thought-life of his day. Now he was a learned Talmudist, and his co-religionists had no fault to find with his ideas of ritual.

The possibility of being a true world-reformer does not depend on occupying any particular position in the thought-world. The possibility of performing that function at all depends on having ideas about the nature of truth which are *living*, in contradistinction to such as are *dead*. The possibility of performing it properly depends on having ideas which are *rhythmic*, in contradistinction to such as are *jerky* or *lawless*. The nearer a man approaches to the possibility of having ideas which combine the characteristics of being

living and of being orderly, the more clearly he sees
that the main object of the founders of Mosaism was to
prepare a race capable of perennially keeping up those
quiet alternations of mental attitude which are the
natural purifiers of all scientific and artistic ideas, and
the thought-equivalent of the rhythmic movements of
the physical heart.

The Pentateuch is the formal ark, which contains, as
a *Shekinah*, the essential ideas of Mosaism.   But one
can never learn any science or art by any amount of
study of even the best text-book, without at least
attempting to work some examples ; least of all can
that most glorious of all arts, the art of organizing
thought, be so learned.   A child's *first* breath is an
effort, and perhaps a painful one ; but after one full
inhalation, the process goes on easily enough ! A rhythm
is always delightful to those who have once got into
the swing of it.   A Jew only needs to get one true conception of what *living truth* means ; he may then attend
to any honest vocation to which he is adapted ; he
simply *cannot help* purifying the thought-life of every
one around him ; the hereditary faculty for doing it is
so ingrained that it goes on without his consciousness.

Orthodox people never seem to see that their singular
dislike to Reformers is of the very same nature as the
dislike of the Egyptians to Moses ; of the professional
scribes to the young teacher who wanted to throw on
old prophecy the light of a living experience gained by
the attempt to realize the prophetic ideal.   It is the
dislike of the Inquisition to Galileo ; of the medical
profession in Harvey's time to the doctrine of the
circulation of the blood ; the dislike of the stagnant

mind to whatever forces it to recognize throughout creation the existence of that incessant rhythmic pulsation which is the appointed purifier of all that is foul, the liberator of all that is enslaved. Only those who doubt the power given to the Ark to keep its own place as the Centre of the world's march, need fear to see its accessories move round it as the earth moves round the Sun.

The method suggested in the Pentateuch for the cultivation of the rhythmic condition of the brain is marvellous in its naïve beauty, and whenever it has been followed *in its simplicity, according to the spirit of the Founders*, it has produced results of which it is not too much to say that they are properly "miraculous," *i.e.,* they are beyond anything which can be explained in words, even by the person who produces them.

The essence of the rhythmic method consisted in accustoming the consciousness of man to follow, by alternations of thought and emotion, the rhythm of all the discoverable periodicities of Nature ; especially those which affect the human organization.

Many Eastern religions embodied this principle to some extent, by reverently following certain of the Nature-rhythms. The founders of Judaism, true to their worship of Unity, seem to have aimed to embody in the education of the people all that were discoverable. The solar and lunar periods were, of course, to be followed. Then, as the Founders knew (what many good hygienists in various ages and countries have discovered) that the human mind requires, for health, a change of occupation and of attitude once in seven days, they did not merely say, as modern doctors do,

"Take a rest regularly once a week"; they thought:
"The fact that there is a *need* for a seven days' rhythm
in the human organization proves that there *is* some
seven days' rhythm in the creative agency by which
man was brought into being." Therefore they made it
a matter not only of hygiene but of religion to mark
the seven days' rhythm by arousing, each week, impressive and solemn forms of consciousness, as a counter-
action to the mechanical drudgery of the other six days.
They also utilized, in a similar manner, the changes in
family life and the epochs of National history. They
felt that as to a man is the regular pulsation of his heart
and lungs, so is, to creative wisdom, the complex
rhythm of Nature; and they thought too (and were
they not right in so thinking?) that nothing is more likely
to put man into *rapport* with living truth than getting
his mind to beat in unison with the heart-beats of the
unseen Father.

The effect, in those comparatively rare instances in
which the discipline was carried out in the true spirit of
the Founders, was something like that which is produced
in the wood of a violin by the constant repetition of
musical notes, or in iron by lying along a magnetic
current. The brain of the best kind of Jew is an instrument which catches the property of rhythmic thought
by constant contact with the periodic movements of
Nature; and at last it becomes an instrument which,
when a set of facts is presented to it, the special laws of
which are as yet unknown, proceeds to deal with them,
spontaneously, according to the laws of Nature and of
Logic. It repeats, at every slightest touch, the true
rhythm of creative truth. Such a real Jew was called,

in old days, a "Prophet." Moses wished that all the Lord's people should be Prophets. There was a hope that some day the education of Prophets should be complete; that absolute incarnation of rhythmic grace and Logic should become possible. But the idea of so tuning feeling and thought into harmony with natural law, that rhythmic laws, hitherto unknown, should re-echo, or reveal themselves, within the brain, was too overwhelming a conception to enter the average Jewish mind; and unfortunately the rhythmic mode of education is liable to become mechanical. The majority of Jews, in all ages, have supposed that there was some special duty or virtue in observing *this* or *that* festival. And, of course, any idolatrous over-tension of this kind impairs mental elasticity, and does away with much of the good result of Jewish discipline. Therefore Judaism has always hitherto been as a frost-bound landscape, illuminated by a few prophetic stars. But modern Science seems now touching it with her magic wand, and crying: "Arise, Shine, for God hath said: 'Let light be'; and the *Shekinah* of the Lord shall be revealed."

Messiah's Kingdom cannot mean the rule of any one Incarnation, past, present, or to come; the possibility of any such autocracy being a source of permanent health or prosperity is precluded by the very form of those equations according to which (whether we are aware of it or not) we must think whenever we think sanely. An embodied perfection, who shall spare other people the trouble of thinking for themselves, by telling them what they are to do and to believe, may be a suitable ideal for cowards; but no such anomaly can be the Messiah, or will be tolerated by the leaders of living Science.

The vicious habit of trying to make God in the likeness of phenomena, instead of remembering that the human mind was created in the likeness of God in order that it might *compare* and *organize* and thus *master* phenomena, has led to this among other grotesque and horrible results:—That because we happen to live in a planetary system, in which only one focal luminary has succeeded in struggling out of the condition of nebulous potentiality into that of coherent fact, men have jumped to the conclusion that this abortive condition of our own home is a law for the whole possible range of Being. Jews in old times, instead of faithfully proclaiming the doctrine of *Invisible Unity*, with all its logical consequences, invented the idea that all Israël, and indeed all Humanity, is to be ruled by one Messiah! and Christians, following suit, have improved on the absurdity of their former teachers, by desiring to extend the dominion of their Messiah to the whole Universe, and make of him the equivalent of God Almighty! Mathematicians, however, who are beginning to spend much of their thought-life in solar systems more complete than our own, the source of whose force is a *polar-relation* between *more than one sun*, are beginning to find that the belief in a phenomenal Almighty is out of line with the most elementary properties of matter and of force, with the first principles of Logic and of Hygiene. The whole idea of *sacred phenomena* is revolting to the fine mathematical instinct. *Love* is sacred; and whoever can make himself loved is legitimately sacred to those who love him. Not any one human King, but Love the Inspirer, shall reign for ever and ever. The Messianic Kingdom will come, when in every town in the world there is some beloved teacher holding a divine commission to give his blessing *urbi et orbi*, by opening the Ark of the Shemang Israël, and revealing the living Shekinah, the rhythmic pulsation of all life and truth. For from Zion shall the Law go forth, and the word of the Lord from Jerusalem. And there is no superstition in believing that a man is *divinely commissioned* to do that which we find him doing unconsciously; no progress in Science need make us doubt that a baby's heart has a divine commission to keep up circulation and vital heat. Wherever a man is found, whose own thought-sequences have caught the true rhythm of the Shemang Israël, other men are found clinging lovingly round him. The time comes, at last, when even the orthodox, weary of the cramping fetters of a system of interpretation untrue to the Laws of Nature, are ready to cry to such a teacher: " Master, to whom should we go? thou hast the words of Eternal Life." And if coming to him is only allowed to mean a temporary rest for the weary and heavy laden, he is as willing to bid them come as the sun is to attract and to enlighten. But his hold on their allegiance will be not static and dead, but living and dynamic. The moment that any idolatrous tension on his personality or his characteristics is set up, the true teacher gives new impulsion to his pupils, sending them forth on their appointed path: " Why call ye me good? There is none good but One, that is God. Call no man your Master on earth; for One is your Master, even The Unseen Unity. And greater work than mine shall my successors do, when I have gone to the Father."

Let us choose this day whom we will serve. Phenomena, classifications, fixed rules, have proved that they are powerless to unify and heal; if The Unseen Unity be God, let us worship Him, and Him only, with all our hearts. The standards of the creeds have been warring against each other, because they have emancipated themselves from their rightful ruler. The Crescent, the symbol of the fatality of Natural Law; the Torah, the standard of obedience to rule; the Trinity, the Ideal of metaphysical classification; the Cross, the witness to the elevation of the despised; the Crucifix, the sublimization of utter adoration; each has aspired to create man in its own image; but man, who is made in the Image of God, has escaped from the control of them all. But now, as in the days of Moses, Science is raising those Natural Symbols which are the pledge of God's power to reveal the law of continuity, and of man's power to reverse the lines of Separation. The Trumpet has sounded to herald the Festival of Nature, when God shall be sought under no roof made with hands, but under the trees which He hath planted. The Water is being poured forth abundantly from the golden ewer.[1] The Spirit of Progress and the Church of Truth say come; let whoever understandeth help to spread the Good News. And let him that is athirst come, and whosoever will, let him take the Water of Life freely.

---

[1] This refers to some ceremonies of the Feast of Tabernacles.

FROM AN ARYAN SEERESS TO A HEBREW PROPHET.

DEATH a Terror?   Your thinking unveiled to my sight!
My heart bare before you in Heaven's own Light!
Our vesture of flesh shed off into the grave,
And nothing between us our love to enslave!
My own personal life has but parted us two;
And its death, O! my love! will be union with you.

Death a Terror?   Yes, surely.   For Love is a Fire.
We children of earth know not what we desire.
The Eternal, in passing us, stretched out His Hand
That we might not be lightning-struck, here, as we stand;
And I think, O! my dear one! 'tis only too true
That THAT HAND put a veil between Gentile and Jew.

Death a Terror?   Ah! yes! of all terrors the King.
Are we fit for such bliss as that meeting may bring?
The dazzle of wonder, the splendour unknown
Of a flash from your soul as it strikes on my own.
Then,——nor female nor male, no more Gentile nor Jew,
No more check on my freedom but union with you.

M

Appendix I

*For those who wish to understand practically the connec-
tion of the method of Gratry and Boole with ancieut
Philosophies.*

INITIATION FOR PHYSIC MATHEMATICS.

LET the aspirant occasionally, when he is in any difficulty, put himself back in imagination into pre-historic
times.   Let him try to fancy himself an early Geologist,
surrounded by savages who ask him to find water.

The Geologist takes the opportunity of showing them
how to find the Water of Life.   He says :—

"Let us seek the Great Father in our spirit ; then
perhaps He will show us how to supply our bodily
needs.

" The truth is holy and pure ; and may not be taught
by any tree that has thorns or the likeness of the horns
or tail of any beast ; but only by this, the Sacred Hazel
(or Olive, etc.).   And let us put out of our minds all
imperfect ideas and animal impulses ; and seek to
understand in straightforward simplicity.

" Separation seems to us an evil; but in reality it is
not so ; it is a condition of growth.   Look at this tree ;
the branch that here has one bark-case, higher up is
divided into two.   It must be so ; without separations
nothing can grow into beauty.   Therefore if God sepa-
rates us from our friends, let us remember that separation
is not an evil but a means of progress.

"Man is, like the trees, subject to the Law of separation ; but he is not, like the trees, its slave.   He is the

son of the Law-giver ; and heir of His power.   I hold
in my hand the instrument of separation ; and can inflict
it on anything that grows."

(He raises a knife.)

" Man, the Son of God, is Lord of all created things,
and should pay superstitious homage to none.   Therefore I fear not to cut this branch, though it grows on
the Sacred Hazel."

(He cuts the branch, and takes it by the two prongs,
the united end hanging downwards.)

" You call me Healer, Teacher and Counsellor ; but
my knowledge resides not in me.   It comes from The
Great Unity ; and I acquire it by putting together in
my mind things which I see dissevered, and dissevering
in my mind things which I see together.   In token
whereof I reverse this branch ; putting Unity where was
division, and division where Unity was."

(He reverses the wand).

" If any of you seek help from me, I bid you come
while I hold reversed this sacred branch of divination ;
in order that you may always remember that knowledge
comes from putting together things which we find separated, and separating things which we find together.

" This knowledge is not mine, to give or to withhold;
it comes down from The Unseen Unity Whose servant
and revealer I am ; and is given, freely, to all who seek
it with a pure heart.   In token whereof I raise this
branch high over your heads and mine."

(He raises the branch.)

"Now lest any should think that the Hazel has powers
of its own, I will cast the branch into the flames, that all
may witness how powerless it is to avert its own disso-

lution.   May the Unseen Father accept the offering of
ourselves and all that we have; and deign to minister
to our bodily needs."

(He burns the branch.)

The awe-struck savages would by this time be polar-
ized into a "circle"; and the Magician (whose Geologic
insight would have been already informed by studious
observation) would become lucid ; and *see* where water
was.

The student should, occasionally, go over this little
scene in his mind; especially when he finds himself in
any intellectual or moral perplexity.   If he holds the
forked stick in his hands and actually goes through the
performance, especially with a freshly-cut stick, so much
the better.   The magnetism of the fresh Hazel-Wand
acts as a slight additional stimulant; much as breathing
doubly oxygenated air for a few minutes might do.

The modern Dowser is one in whom fidelity to the
Past is a *physical* instinct.   When he goes through half
of this ceremony, his fingers tingle with the longing to
complete it.   They and the Hazel mutually magnetize
each other, till the fork, of its own accord, completes as
much of the ceremony as it can.

The Psychic mathematician is one in whom fidelity
to the Past is a *spiritual* instinct.   When he meditates
on old Ceremonies, secrets connected with the mathematical organization of thought reveal themselves
in his brain.   To him, what others call Time is
as a fourth dimension of Space ; and he *sees* it,
stretched out like a line.   His Trinity is not three
Persons in One God, but three times in One Eternal,
Past, Present, and Future.   And when he becomes

lucid, Time becomes foreshortened, and he sees them as One; sees them (at his best) with equal distinctness and assurance.

When the aspirant has become impregnated with the ideas suggested by the early and savage ceremony, he may take a further step. Let him picture a band of eager lovers of Liberty using the Ceremony to initiate a new member. The initiator concludes it by holding the rod by its tips and making it slowly revolve; having the united end alternately above and below his fingers, saying :—

" I dedicate you to the cause of orderly Revolution; and the overthrow of all systems based on the maintenance of any fixed condition of things. Let us pray that the Will of God may be done on earth *as it is in the Heavens;* that is to say, by incessant, orderly Revolution.

"In the Name of The Invisible Unity, Eternal and Inconceivable, Amen."

Let the aspirant go over this in his mind, when he is puzzled by any political or social problem, and fix his mind's eye on the spiral earth-path or moon-path. After a time, he will think of things as Boole and Gratry did, and understand their terminology easily.

An objection has been made to my presentment of the Branch ritual, because old documents prove that Ritual to have been, at various times, connected with fleshly and sensuous ideas. It certainly was so. Those who consider that fact a disproof of my view must have approached the study of ancient systems from the out-side and with minds saturated with European ideas of classification and distinction. The true line of cleavage between good and bad, in religion, lies not between this and that ritual, but between the simple and the perverted use of the same ritual. A Water-Dowser taught me the traditional method of cutting and handling the forked Divining-Rod; and I have no hesitation in affirming that what I witnessed was the remains of some old and very solemn ceremony. I went through the performances repeatedly with the Hazel as instructed by the Dowser; the forks were nearly all plain forked sticks. Afterwards I cut forks from all kinds of shrubs and trees growing in the neighbourhood of Greenstreet (Kent). I got a large collection. Some were like the horns of beetles, oxen, or stags; several would serve for Phallus symbols. One (from a hawthorn) had a thorn out in front and a longer one behind; and bore the most extraordinary resemblance to the hind quarters of an ape in a very nasty attitude. One, from a Honeysuckle, showed a perfect clean fork, a miniature copy of the pure Hazel fork, but with a spiral coil winding round and round it—a perfect picture of the Serpent in the Tree of Knowledge.

This inference illustrates how easily the symbols of a pure religion may slip over into being symbols of degrading idolatry; and how unwise it would be to treat any ancient ritual as in itself and necessarily evil, only because priests have perverted it. This is more especially the case, because the Creator Inspirer, Who descends at the moment of contact between differentiated polars, is the object of worship of all inspired Genius. Adonis,—the god of vicious wasteful expenditure of force in the pursuit of mere sensuous pleasure, is the same word as Adonai, the Fertilizing Inspirer of the

Hebrew; the name too sacred to be written and indicated only by dots. Pan, the horrible Satyr, is "the All," the Unity of Nature; identical with "The I Am, the Unity" Who delivered Israël from bondage.

FORMULA FOR SOCIAL COMBINATION

THE maximum of force is got by a coalition between the party rising into predominance and the class most neglected and despised.   In France, in the 18th century, Philosophy was the rising power, and the proletariat were almost deprived of Civil rights; when they combined, they swept everything before them.   In England, now, Science, especially psychological Science, is the rising power, and the only class denied all right is the class of lunatics.

Appendix II

WHATEVER may be the faults of the Jewish people, a question which need not be here discussed, they have brought down to us from some remote civilization a tradition of enormous value :—

The vital conviction which, during thousands of years, at all times pressed upon the Israëlites, was that they were a "chosen people" selected out of all the multitudes of the earth to perpetuate the great truth that there was but one God—an illimitable, omnipotent, paternal spirit who rewarded the good and punished the wicked—in contradistinction from the multifarious subordinate animal and bestial demi-gods of the other nations of the earth. This sublime monotheism could only have been the outgrowth of a high civilization, for man's first religion is necessarily a worship of "stocks and stones," and history teaches us that the gods decrease in number as man increases in intelligence. It was probably in Atlantis that monotheism was first preached. The proverbs of "Ptah-hotep," the oldest book of the Egyptians, show that this most ancient colony from Atlantis received the pure faith from the motherland at the very dawn of history : this book preached the doctrine of *one* God, " the rewarder of the good and the punisher of the wicked." (Reginald S. Poole, *Contemporary Review*, Aug., 1881, p. 38.) "In the early days the Egyptians worshipped one only God, the maker of all things, without beginning and without end. To the last the priests preserved this doctrine and taught it privately to a select few." (*Amer. Ency.*, vol. vi. p. 463.) The Jews took up this great truth where the Egyptians dropped it, and over the heads and over the ruins of Egypt, Chaldea, Phœnicia, Greece, Rome, and India this handful of poor shepherds,—ignorant, debased, and despised,—have carried down to our times a conception which could only have originated in the highest possible state of human society.

And even scepticism must pause before the miracle of the continued existence of this strange people, wading through the ages, bearing on their shoulders the burden of their great trust, and pressing forward under the force of a perpetual and irresistible impulse. The speech that may be heard to-day in the synagogues of Chicago and Melbourne, resounded two thousand years ago in the streets of Rome; and at a still earlier period, it could be heard in the palaces of Babylon and the shops of Thebes—in Tyre, in Sidon, in Gades, in Palmyra, in Nineveh. How many nations have perished, how many languages have ceased to exist, how many splendid civilizations have crumbled into ruin, how many temples and towers and towns have gone down into dust since the sublime frenzy of monotheism first seized this extraordinary people? All their kindred nomadic tribes have gone; their land of promise is in the hands of strangers; but Judaism, with its offspring, Christianity, is taking possession of the habitable world; and the continuous life of one people—one poor, obscure, and wretched people—spans the tremendous gulf between " Ptah-hotep " and this nineteenth century.

If the Spirit of which the universe is but an expression —of whose frame the stars are the infinite molecules—

can be supposed ever to interfere with the laws of matter and reach down into the doings of men, would it not be to save from the wreck and waste of time the most sublime fruit of the civilization of the drowned Atlantis —a belief in the one, only, just God, the father of all life, the imposer of all moral obligations?

Printed by S. CLARKE,
Granby Row, Manchester.

THE

WORLD'S RELIGION SERIES.

BY W. LOFTUS HARE.

*Foolscap 8vo   64 pp.   Artistic cover.   6d. net each.
By post, 7d.*

I. RELIGION.

Being an exposition of the Philosophy of Universal Religion, of which the remaining volumes are concrete examples.

II. HINDOO RELIGION.

Chiefly a study of the prevailing Brahmanic Doctrines of Sankhya, Yoga, and Vedanta.

III. GREEK RELIGION.

A brief study of early Greek Theology and its diverging philosophical doctrines: Socrates, Plato, Plotinos, and the Stoics.

*IV. BABYLONIAN RELIGION.

A study of the ancient Science and Theology of Chaldeans and Assyrians, pointing out their relation to Jewish religious history and religious literature.

V. THE RELIGION OF THE JEWS.

A study of the Jewish pre-Christian religion and literature and history, together with a sketch of modern belief.

VI. CHRISTIANITY.

A study of the teaching of Jesus the Christ; the true nature of His message; together with a statement of the contribution of Paul to the Christian doctrine.

*Other volumes by the same Author are also
in preparation.*

LONDON : C. W. DANIEL, 3 AMEN CORNER, E.C.

THE CHRISTIAN MYSTICS:

A Series of Sketches of the Lives and
Works of some Leaders of Christian
Thought.

BY W. P. SWAINSON.

I. FRANCIS OF ASSISI:
Saint and Mystic.

II. EMMANUEL SWEDENBORG:
The Swedish Seer.

III. GEORGE FOX:
The English Quaker.

IV. MADAME GUYON:
The French Quietist.

V. JACOB BOEHME:
The God-taught Philosopher.

VI. JOHN TAULER:
The Friend of God.

VII. PARACELSUS:
Mediæval Alchemist.

*Artistic Paper Covers, 3d. each; by post, 3½d.
The first Six Numbers in Two Vols., Cloth,
1s. 6d. net per Vol.; by post, 1s. 7d.*

LONDON: C. W. DANIEL, 3 AMEN CORNER, E.C.

LOGIC TAUGHT BY LOVE.

Rhythm in Nature and in Education. By MARY EVEREST BOOLE. Crown 8vo, cloth, 3s. 6d. net.

THE GREATER PARABLES OF TOLSTOY,

With their Interpretation, as told to his Congregation. By WALTER WALSH. Crown 8vo, cloth, 2s. net; paper covers, 1s. net.

TARIFF WITHOUT TEARS.

A Primer of Taxation. Written and Illustrated by HAROLD E. HARE. Cloth, 1s. 6d. net.

CRUMBS OF VERSE,

Mainly for Chicks. By J. H. GORING, and Illustrations by EVELYN PAUL. New Cloth Edition, 1s. net.

BERTHA STORIES,

And Stories told by her Uncle Gilbert. By G. G. DESMOND, and Nine Illustrations by EVELYN PAUL. New Cloth Edition, 1s. net.

LONDON: C. W. DANIEL, 3 Amen Corner, E.C

This book is **DUE** on the last date stamped below

Form L-9—15m-7,'31